THE DYNAMICS OF CONGRESS
THE GUIDE TO THE PEOPLE AND PROCESS OF LAWMAKING

PATRICIA D. WOODS, PHD
THE WOODS INSTITUTE

The Woods Institute offers seminars for businesses and organizations that need to understand the legislative operations in the U.S. Congress and the state, local, and national government relations within the federal system. Programs are tailored to the interests of the participants. Speakers and course materials are chosen to meet the client's needs. Members of Congress and their staffs, elected state and local officials, journalists, and government scholars are among the speakers who participate in the Institute's programs. Clients have included Aerospatiale, Bureau of Land Management, Georgetown University, McDonnell Douglas Corporation, National Association of Counties, National Park Service, Naval Air Systems Command, Naval Test Pilot School, Office of Inspector General (Department of Defense), U.S. Conference of Mayors, U.S. Department of State, U.S. Fish and Wildlife Service, USDA Forest Service, U.S. Information Agency, and the University of Virginia.

ISBN 9781456473259

Additional copies may be purchased from

The Woods Institute
2231 California St., N.W., #603
Washington, DC 20008
(202) 483-6167
Email: pwoods@woodsinstitute.com
www.woodsinstitute.com

Printed in the United States of America

Acknowledgements

This 10th Edition of Dynamics of Congress could not have happened without the valuable help and input from several very important people. I wanted to try to "tech up" the book while staying true to its content. My executive assistant, Nancy Metry, created the design of the book as well as the layout. Her computer knowledge and expertise made this edition possible. Mary Ann Baer provided the final edit with great care. Matt Ketman, a congressional staff assistant for my congressman, Chris Van Hollen, Jr. helped update the important chapter on accessing Capitol Hill. Many thanks to each of them.

Any errors in the content of the book are entirely mine.

WOODS INSTITUTE SERVICE PROFILE

The Woods Institute of Washington, D.C., offers seminars for businesses and organizations that need to know about the legislative operations in the U.S. Congress as well as the state, local, and national government relations within the federal system. Speakers and course materials are chosen to meet a client's needs. Members of Congress and their staffs, elected state and local officials, journalists, and government scholars are among the speakers who participate in the institute's programs. Clients have included the U.S. Forest Service, the National Park Service, Bureau of Land Management, the U.S. Fish and Wildlife Service, the Bureau of Indian Affairs, Department of State, Naval Test Pilot School, Naval Air Systems Command, U.S. Information Agency, National Association of Counties, Conference of Mayors, Georgetown University, Trinity University of Washington, D.C., University of Virginia, Aerospatiale, Matras, Association of American Residents Overseas and McDonnell-Douglas Corporation.

Dr. Patricia D. Woods, director of the institute, has nearly 20 years of experience working at the federal, state, and local levels. More than 15,000 executives, managers, and support staff from 50 federal agencies and private industry have participated in her courses. Prior to the establishment of the Woods Institute, she was a visiting professor with the Government Affairs Institute of the Office of Personnel Management in Washington, D.C., where she lectured on the Congress, the federal budget and the economy, legislative tracking, and federalism. Comments on her courses have included the following: *"I should have had this course when I first entered the federal government," "I now have a greater awareness of the budget and legislation affecting my job," "All Americans should take this course on the Congress," "I have a better understanding of the pressures that face elected officials,"* and *"An outstanding macro view of the Pentagon budget process."*

Her expertise in state and local government comes from more than seven years with the Louisiana Legislature in Baton Rouge and the National Association of Counties in Washington, D.C.

Curriculum

The institute's curriculum includes seminars on:

- The Congressional Committee Hearing Process: Testifying Before Congress

- Congressional Operations: A Study of the U.S. Congress

- Congress and Elections

- The Federal Budget and the Congressional Budget Process

- The Defense Budget Process in the Washington Community

- The Washington Foreign Policy Process

- Federalism: Intergovernmental Relations in the Federal System

- Federal Government Operations

- Selected Topics in American History and Government

TABLE OF CONTENTS

x

INTRODUCTION

Many changes have occurred in accessing and following the procedures on Capitol Hill since the first edition of *Dynamics of Congress* appeared in 1984. Up until 1995 very few members of Congress had websites and practically no one used the Internet as a way to provide and access information on Capitol Hill. When Newt Gingrich became speaker of the House of Representatives in 1995, he encouraged the expansion of the digital age on Capitol Hill with the establishment of **thomas.gov**, a website of the Library of Congress that provides a wealth of information for the American citizens about legislative action on Capitol Hill.

As the updating of the 10th edition of *Dynamics of Congress* in 2011 is taking place, the use of the Internet, websites, You Tube, Twitter and many other social media and network websites has greatly expanded among the American people and across the globe. There are many ways to access the workings of Capitol Hill - from paid subscriptions to non-governmental organizations and think tanks to government sources as well. I have decided to focus on three sites that will help you connect with the digital U.S. Congress as you read the text of *Dynamics of Congress*. You have paid for these sites with your tax dollars so you might as well use them!

By using **house.gov**, **senate.gov** and **thomas.gov**, you will have up-to-date information on current action on Capitol Hill.

On the following pages you will find the home pages for these sites. Periodically throughout the book we will visit these sites through exercises to familiarize you with the location and navigation styles of each website. The hard copy text may use the web references to follow up to research topics or track bills.

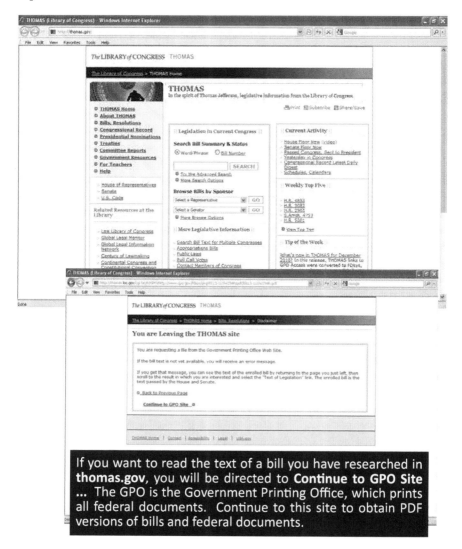

If you want to read the text of a bill you have researched in **thomas.gov**, you will be directed to **Continue to GPO Site** ... The GPO is the Government Printing Office, which prints all federal documents. Continue to this site to obtain PDF versions of bills and federal documents.

But more important than the technological changes on Capitol Hill since 1984 has been the change in politics of the Members of Congress. Members of both the House and the Senate in recent years from both the Republican and Democratic parties have refused to compromise, to negotiate, to form a consensus, elements at the heart of a representative democracy's policy-making process. Such intractability has resulted in a gridlock for law making, the argument over the fiscal cliff in late 2012 being the latest example. The key to this inability of Congress to act may just be the American people themselves who have the government they want in the entitlement, domestic, and national security programs but are unwilling to pay for them.

How a Bill Becomes a Law

To understand the legislative process is to understand the nature of the U.S. Congress. It is the only democratically elected national assembly in the world that both represents and legislates. These two hats worn by senators and representatives must be kept in mind when the outside observer of a seemingly chaotic Congress offers the criticism that "nothing ever gets done on Capitol Hill."

One of the reasons that Congress "works" is because it does not work smoothly. Congress was meant to be a deliberative body. This slow process of lawmaking has resulted in a government that has remained free from tyranny for more than 200 years.

Members of the U.S. Congress hold their seats because they are elected by "the people back home" who expect their interests to be represented at

the national level. A senator represents an entire state while a House member represents a district of between 500,000 and 800,000 people. Answering to a constituency group every two (House) or six (Senate) years ensures that members of Congress keep the interests of their states and districts in mind when they put on the lawmaker's hat. In fact, much of the legislation drafted and eventually signed into law closely reflects the needs and interests of the voters throughout the country.

At the beginning of each new Congress - in early January in the odd-numbered calendar years - bills and resolutions are introduced in both the House and the Senate. (The 112th Congress was sworn in on January 5, 2011.) As many as 10,000 pieces of legislation may be submitted for consideration over the next two years, the length of each Congress. Proposed laws may relate to issues ranging from pollution to obesity to increased homeland security to import duties to gun control.

Congress is a bicameral legislature, and all bills must pass both the House and the Senate before being signed into law by the President. When the bills are dropped into the hopper in each chamber, the "grinding" process for the final product begins. The "flow chart" on the following page describes the process. At the beginning of the 112th Congress in 2011

The Course of Legislation

Code of a Bill

H.R./S.	1/336	(111)
Introduced in House or Senate	Order in which bill was received	Congress

HOUSE
- ▶ H.R. 1 introduced
- ▶ Referred to committee then to subcommittee
- ▶ Subcommittee hearings and markup
- ▶ Subcommittee approves H.R. 1
- ▶ Committee consideration
- ▶ Committee reports out H.R. 1
- ▶ Committee report filed
- ▶ Rules Committee decides to move H.R. 1
- ▶ House amends and passes H.R. 1
- ▶ House requests conference • •

Senate
- ▶ S. 336 introduced
- ▶ Referred to committee then to subcommittee
- ▶ Subcommittee hearings and markup
- ▶ Subcommittee approves S. 336
- ▶ Committee consideration
- ▶ Committee reports out S. 336
- ▶ Committee report filed
- ▶ Senate amends and passes S. 336
- ▶ Senate agrees to conference

▶ Conference on H.R. 1 and S. 336

▶ Conference report filed

House adopts report   ▶ Senate adopts report

▶ Enrollment

▶ *President signs H.R. 1/S. 336 = P.L. 101-16*

Code of a Public Law

P.L.	111	16
Public Law	Congressional Session	Number of law passed

the republican majority in the House made several rules changes. One of them stated that any new legislation needed to contain a "Constitutional Authority" statement. The statement must show the specific part of the Constitution that empowers Congress to enact legislation.

The parliamentarians of the House and the Senate together with the leadership in each house refer the bill to the designated standing committee that has jurisdiction over the issue. For example, all social security legislation is referred to the Committee on Finance in the Senate and to the Committee on Ways and Means in the House. Each of these committees has a special subcommittee to review all legislation on social security. Falling under a clear jurisdiction of only one committee or subcommittee in each house of Congress greatly eases a bill's progress through the legislative process.

Much legislation does not receive such straightforward referral to committee. The leadership may determine that a bill addresses a variety of issue areas; thus, the legislation moves through the slow process of examination by several committees and subcommittees. Other means of referral include split referral and sequential referral (see the Glossary in the Appendix section for an explanation of these terms).

Joint referral has been eliminated in the House. An example of how legislation can be bogged down because of overlapping committee jurisdiction was the North American Free Trade Agreement in 1993 which was considered by over a half a dozen committees and subcommittees in the House.

COMMITTEE ACTION

Just because a bill is introduced and referred to committee does not mean that it will ever move to the hearing stage since the hearings usually begin at the subcommittee level. Most legislation "dies" in committee from lack of interest.

EXERCISE: Bills Introduced in Current Congress

- Go to **thomas.gov**
- In the middle column, you can search for a bill in the Current Congress by **Word/Phrase**, **Bill Number**, **Representative** or **Senator**.
- Select your Congressional Representative or Senator(s) from the drop down list. You will be taken to a new screen that lists all of the bills they sponsored in the current congress. Click **GO**.

Example: Representative John Boehner (R-OH), sponsored 17 Bills in the 111th Congress.

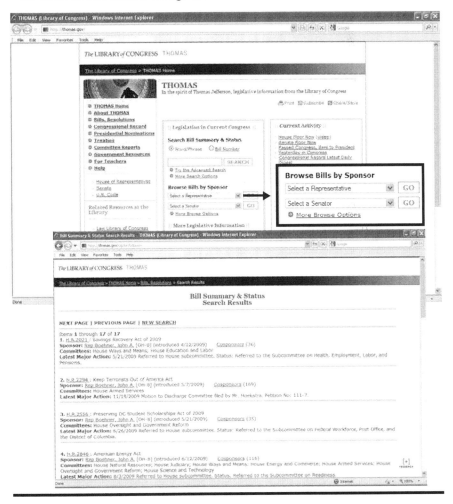

One of the real challenges on Capitol Hill is to generate interest in an issue and get a hearing scheduled. Holding press conferences, writing letters to other members, obtaining letters and emails from voters, gaining presidential interest and activating public or private interest groups are all tactics that a representative or senator can use to get a hearing on his or her bill.

Finally, generating the interest of the subcommittee chairperson is another crucial means. If the chairperson decides to conduct a hearing, some of the witnesses from his or her district may be invited to testify. The power of the chairpersons of these committees and subcommittees also is wielded by scheduling, or not scheduling, hearings and by inviting favorable or opposing witnesses to testify.

After all testimony is gathered, the subcommittee, with the help of its staff, begins the "markup." At this point the real crafting of legislation

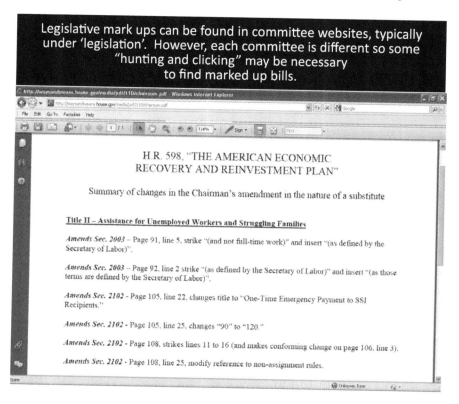

begins as amendments to change the bill are offered by committee members. These sessions are often referred to as 'mark ups".

Now is when the work of lobbyists, interest groups and executive agency personnel who favor or oppose the bill, may or may not pay off. Finding a subcommittee member or members to sponsor an amendment to a piece of legislation generally describes a large part of the work of thousands of people, the lobbyists, who roam the halls on Capitol Hill.

Amendments agreed to in subcommittee are incorporated into the bill that, on final vote, is reported to the full committee. At the full committee level additional hearings may be held and more amendments may be offered. If, for instance, a lobbying group failed to have an amendment adopted in subcommittee, it can try to find other sponsoring members on the full committee. Again, however, the power and interest of the chairperson can be seen in his or her ability to schedule hearings on legislation. In the recent 110th and 111th Congresses, Democratic chairpersons in both the House and the Senate have agreed on most legislation coming out of the subcommittees and have not obstructed full committee consideration. This does not mean, however, that a chairperson could refuse to hold hearings on a bill.

A new rule passed by the republican controlled House in January 2011 for the 112th Congress states that the text of the legislation must be posted on a Committee's website 24 hours prior to a mark up. The House Rules Committee has been exempted.

FLOOR CONSIDERATION

When a bill is approved by the full committee in the Senate, the bill's sponsor works with the leadership to schedule floor consideration. Being a smaller body the Senate operates very much like a club whose 100 members "unanimously consent" to the proceedings in their chamber. The Senate

---

Exercise: Congressional Hearings
- Go to **house.gov.**
- In the "Committees' Web sites (A-Z), select **Committee on Energy and Commerce** from the drop down list. Click **GO**.
- On the Committee's Web page, float over the **Hearings** link on the menu bar.
- Select **Subcommittee on Commerce, Trade, and Consumer Protection**. This site lists recent hearings on proposed bills.
- Click **Read more...** on any of the legislation to get a list of witnesses and links to related documents.

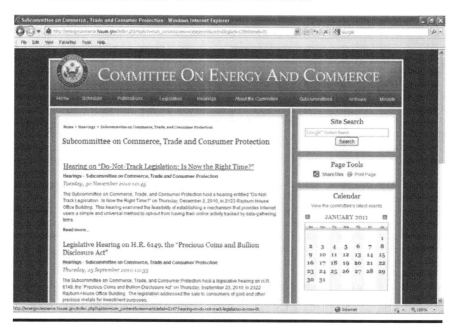

leadership takes into account the senators' meeting schedules, speaking engagements and travel plans in an effort to arrange for the Senate's business to be transacted in accordance with the membership's wishes.

Indeed, this informality spills over onto the Senate floor when debate on the proposed law takes place. Unlike the House amendments, both germane and non-germane, may be offered from the floor by any senator at any time. Debate is unlimited in the Senate but not in the House.

In the 109th Congress, the Senate considered abolishing the filibuster on the President's judicial nominees, but a bi-partisan compromise was reached that resulted in the continuity of the filibuster in the Senate.

The use or threat of the use of the filibuster has greatly slowed the work of the Senate in recent years. Because a vote of 60 senators, referred to as a cloture vote, is needed to stop a filibuster or unlimited debate on any matter that may come before the Senate, the minority party may use this weapon to obstruct Senate business. Between 2007 and 2010 when the Democrats controlled the Senate, the Republicans threatened a filibuster more that 380 times, 130 in the 110th Congress (2007-2008) and over 275 times in the 111th Congress (2009-2010). Since the Democrats had a majority of 60 votes for only about six months in 2009, the Republicans successfully slowed or stopped legislative initiatives supported by the Obama administration and Democratic senators.

> **filibuster**
> Informal term for any attempt to block or delay Senate action on a bill or other matter by debating it at length, by offering numerous procedural motions or by any other delaying or obstructive actions.

As of this revision of the Dynamics of Congress, the Senate in the 112th Congress (2011) is considering some rules changes regarding the filibuster that will enable more timely consideration of bills on the Senate floor.

A far less casual arrangement exists in the House of Representatives, a legislative body consisting of 441 (435 elected state representatives and six delegates) men and women. Ordinarily, when a bill is voted out of committee in the House, it is placed on a legislative schedule called a calendar. Although having successfully been heard and approved by committee much legislation dies on the calendar because there is not enough time to consider the bill. (Remember that about 10,000 pieces of legislation are introduced in each Congress, a period of two years, with fewer than 600 being signed into law by the President.)

To ensure the consideration of important legislation in the House the Rules Committee acts as the "traffic cop" over the flow of legislation to the House floor (**rules.house.gov**). Sponsors of bills appear before this committee, which is closely allied with the House leadership, to petition for a special rule on when and how their bills will be considered by the full House. This committee determines how long the debate will be, how many, if any, floor amendments will be considered and when final passage will occur.

The will and power of the Speaker of the House to control House business are reflected in this committee. To further control debate on the House floor, the Rules Committee in recent years, whether controlled by the Republicans or the Democrats, has limited the minority party's participation in floor debate. Declaring that no amendments may be offered, a closed rule, or limiting the number of amendments to be offered by the minority, has resulted in even greater control of the House by the majority party.

"*The speaker likes surprises only on his birthday and not on the floor of the House*," responded one staffer of a former speaker when discussing the role of the Rules Committee. Thus, what the "program" for final passage will be in the House of Representatives is well defined before the legislation moves to the floor for a vote. It would make no sense, nor would there be much order, if House rules permitted the 435 voting members to offer any floor amendment at any time. (Note: A rules change in Republican controlled House of Representatives in the 112th Congress now states that the six "delegates" who represent American Samoa, the District of Columbia, Guam, the Northern Mariana Islands, Puerto Rico, and the Virgin Islands may vote *neither* in committee *nor* on the House floor.)

CONFERENCE STAGE: *THE WAY IT WAS*

When a bill has finally passed by a simple majority in both chambers (sometimes this takes 10 to 12 congresses and more than 20 years as in the case of the copyright law), the differences between the House and Senate versions of the bill must be resolved in conference committee. The art of compromise in the legislative process is still being exercised at this final, very important, stage.

Selection of Conferees

The Speaker of the House and the Senate Majority Leader and the chairperson and ranking minority member of the committees that heard the bill select the House and Senate members who are to serve as conferees. Generally speaking, these committee leaders choose members on their own committees and subcommittees. Sometimes, however, if someone is a known expert on the subject and is not a member of the committee, he or she will also be selected. Conference committees are often larger. For example, in 1996, the conference committee for the immigration bill had more than 50 members. In recent years, participation by the minority (the Democrats) in conference committees was limited by the majority (the Republicans) in the case of the Medicare Reform Bill passed in 2003.

Conference Negotiations

In this final stage of the legislative process, lobbyists, the political action committees (PACs), "the people back home" and the White House have one more chance to influence the final language of the bill that the President will sign into law. Sometimes legislation that is strongly supported even by a President dies in conference.

This conference stage may last a few hours, several weeks or many months. Although the conference chairperson is chosen in an ad hoc fashion, he or she influences the scheduling and pace of the conference and its bargaining negotiations. The staff also participates in the conference process by drafting amendments, working out agreements and writing the final conference report.

When the committee, the "final court of appeals," has reached agreement, the conference bill and report must be approved by both the House and the Senate. The bill cannot be amended on the floor but rules in the House grant prerogative motions authorizing committee chairpersons to make an objection if they oppose legislative or authorizing language inserted in appropriations bills by the Senate or a conference committee. Authorizing chairpersons can debate on the House floor any language they oppose.

Rejection of the report by either chamber means that the bill has failed to pass. Depending on the importance of the legislation, the bill either dies or is returned to the conference committee for reconsideration. Acceptance by both houses through a simple majority vote means that the bill has passed and is ready for the President's signature.

THE CONFERENCE STAGE: *THE WAY IT IS*

In the late 1990s and early 2000s when the Republicans controlled the House of Representatives, participation by the minority (the Democrats) in conference committees began to be limited by the majority (the Republicans). A good example was the Medicare Reform bill of 2003 conference that resulted in very little input by the Democrats. When the Democrats took control of the House again in 2007, their leadership talked about greater inclusion of the Republicans, then the minority, in conference committees. Reality has proven otherwise. Twenty years ago, from 1989-1991, there were 44 non-appropriations bills reported by conference. In the recent 111th Congress, there were only two, a bill concerning Iran and the financial reform legislation. Conference reports can be viewed in **thomas.gov** by clicking on **Committee Reports** on the left side, then under **Browse Committee Reports by**, select **Conference**.

Current Conferees and Conference Negotiations

To better manage legislation these days House and Senate majority leaders as well as the committee chairpersons act as conferees to negotiate the final bill. Since no formal committee has been appointed, the House and Senate leadership makes deals for final bills behind closed doors. Different versions of the legislation with added amendments are sent back and forth between chambers, known as "the ping-pong process", until a final version for a law is reached.

This process began when the Republicans took control of Congress in 1995 and has continued under the Democrats with Nancy Pelosi as Speaker of the House and Harry Reid as Senate Majority Leader. Both parties when in the majority have argued that the conference committee would be abused by the majority to slow down the legislative process. Has the American democratic process lost something of openness and transparency?

Actual Bill Through Legislative Process
109th Congress and the
Caribbean National Forest Act of 2005

A bill to designate certain National Forest System land in the Commonwealth of Puerto Rico as components of the National Wilderness Preservation System, H.R. 539, was introduced into the House of Representatives. After receiving consideration by a subcommittee and a committee, it was passed by the House and sent to the Senate. After Senate committee consideration, H.R. 539 was passed and signed into law by the President in January of 2006. There was no conference on the legislation.

2005   HOUSE

February 2 ⇒ H.R. 539 introduced

June 14 ⇒ Reported on by Committee on Resources

Sept. 13 ⇒ H.R. 539 passes House

SENATE

Sept. 14 ⇒ H.R. 539 received in Senate

October 19 ⇒ Energy and Natural Resources Committee reports on H.R. 539

Nov. 16 ⇒ H.R. 539 passes Senate*

PRESIDENT

December 1 ⇒ President signs P.L. 109-118

*There is no Rules Committee in the Senate. A ruling of unanimous consent brings a bill to the floor of the Senate.

THE PRESIDENT'S ROLE

Under the Constitution, the President, as leader of the executive branch of the U.S. Government, may veto any law passed by Congress. However, a veto can be overridden by a two-thirds vote of the active membership in each house of Congress. President George H.W. Bush vetoed 46 bills that the Democratically controlled 101st and 102nd Congresses were unable to override. In contrast to Bush, President Bill Clinton vetoed 36 bills passed by the Republican controlled Congresses during the last six years of his presidency. In his first term, President George W. Bush vetoed no bills passed by the Republican-controlled Congress. A powerful weapon of the presidency, the President's veto pen has prevailed more than 90% of the time since 1989. A Presidential Statement sometimes accompanies either a bill's signing or veto. Go to whitehouse.gov and search by the bill number (i.e. H.R. 1105) to see a Presidential Statement.

THE SUPREME COURT'S ROLE

The Judicial Branch - in addition to the Executive Branch and Congress as the Legislative Branch - can also be a player in the legislative process. In the early years of the Republic the right of judicial review by the Supreme Court of congressionally passed legislation was established by Supreme Court Justice John Marshall in a famous case, *Marbury vs. Madison.* The Constitution does not specifically state that the nation's highest court of law could declare as unconstitutional the laws passed by Congress and signed by the President. The 1803 decision on this case, however, set the precedent for judicial review. The third branch of government, the judiciary, can affect the legislative process by declaring legislation unconstitutional.

SUMMARY

In the high-tech world of the 21st Century, the process that has been outlined appears to be quite inefficient and impractical. Indeed, if robots instead of people were involved, perhaps more work would take place more smoothly on Capitol Hill. However, its sensitivity to the needs of American society makes Congress the truly multidimensional and traditional institution that the founding fathers of this country intended more than 200 years ago.

NOTES

Notes

LEADERSHIP AND OTHER POWER CENTERS IN THE U.S. CONGRESS

N owhere is the presence of a political party felt more in the U.S. Congress than in its leadership and organization. At the beginning of each Congress the members of each party in the Senate and the House choose the people who will lead them over the next two years, the life of a Congress. Not only do both the majority and minority parties select their leaders, but also the party organizations are involved in committee assignments. So for purposes of "setting up house" the parties' role is important. However, any notion of parliamentary or party government stops here.

Alongside the activities of the political parties is the independence of the members of Congress whose primary loyalties are to their constituents, the voters back home. Although the members appreciate leadership and the party when they receive committee assignments that will aid in their reelection, they cease to tow the party line on legislation that is not supported by their constituents. Indeed, the party leadership on Capitol Hill being faced with the strong parochial interests of its membership together with the other bases of power on the Hill has prompted one political scientist to observe, "Congress is organized, but it is not led."

LEADERSHIP ON CAPITOL HILL

The Constitution requires a speaker of the House of Representatives and a president and a president pro tempore in the Senate. Over the years other leadership positions - namely the majority and minority leaders and the majority and the minority whips - have evolved in both these bodies. This is diagramed in the following page. Chief among the duties of these leaders is to work for party unity in accomplishing their legislative agendas in the face of fierce local loyalties. Along with their leadership responsibilities comes the benefits of larger staffs and office space, higher salaries, priority in recognition on the House or Senate

---

EXERCISE: House Leadership in the Constitution

- Go to usconstitution.net
- Click **Single-page** under The United States Constitution; The Text
- Scroll down and Click **Article 1, Section 2 - The House**

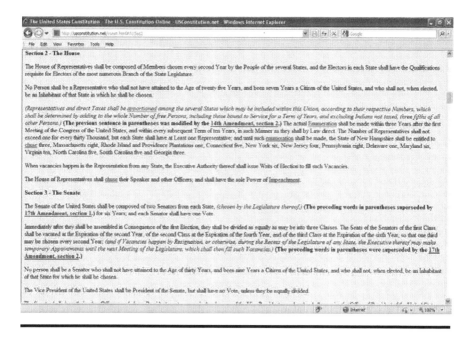

Leadership on Capitol Hill

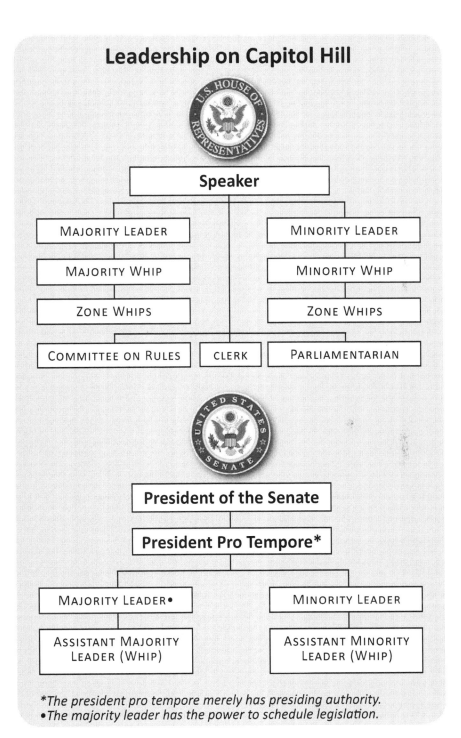

Speaker

MAJORITY LEADER · MINORITY LEADER

MAJORITY WHIP · MINORITY WHIP

ZONE WHIPS · ZONE WHIPS

COMMITTEE ON RULES · CLERK · PARLIAMENTARIAN

President of the Senate

President Pro Tempore*

MAJORITY LEADER• · MINORITY LEADER

ASSISTANT MAJORITY LEADER (WHIP) · ASSISTANT MINORITY LEADER (WHIP)

*The president pro tempore merely has presiding authority.
•The majority leader has the power to schedule legislation.

floor and greater media attention. These leaders, especially the Speaker of the House and the Senate Majority Leader, attend many meetings at the White House and appear frequently on the national news to discuss various congressional activities.

Leaders in the House of Representatives
The Speaker

Although the Constitution does not require the Speaker to come from the House membership, every Speaker has been an elected member of that body. Second in line for the office of President of the United States, after the vice president, is the Speaker of the House of Representatives who often enjoys the most visibility of any leader on Capitol Hill. The 435 House members who can vote on the House floor elect this powerful figure, but this vote is pro forma since choice is strictly along party lines. Prior to the 104th Congress, the Democrats held the position of Speaker for 40 years, from 1955 to 1995. With the congressional elections of 1994, however, the voters elected a majority of Republicans to the House of Representatives. Newt Gingrich of Georgia was elected Speaker. From 1995 to 2006, the Republicans controlled the House of Representatives. Dennis Hastert of Illinois succeeded Gingrich as the Republican Speaker in 1998 when the party lost many House seats in that year's midterm elections. In 2006 the Democrats regained control of the House and elected Nancy Pelosi (D-CA) the first female Speaker of the House. She held this position until the 2010 midterm elections resulted in the Republicans regaining the House with John Boehner of Ohio (R-OH) becoming the Speaker.

While the real power in the House was held by committee chairpersons during most of the twentieth century, the position of Speaker has become more influential and dominant in the activities of the House of Representatives in the 21st century. Beginning in the mid-1970s, the Democratic Speaker became chairperson of the party's Steering and Policy Committee, which assigned Democrats to committees. The Speaker also began to appoint Democratic members to the House Rules Committee, the "traffic cop" that decides which bills will be considered by the full House. Finally, the Speaker, guided by the House parliamentarian, acquired the power to refer bills to several committees which can stall and ultimately derail legislation. In the 21st century, whether a Republican or a Democratic speaker has controlled the House, the speaker has retained these powers.

In the 104th Congress, Speaker Gingrich controlled committee assignments as well as committee chair appointments through the Republican Steering Committee. He also controlled the committees' agendas during those two years as well. But by the middle of the 105th Congress the committee chairpersons had once again asserted their traditional independence from the Speaker.

In contrast to the fragmented nature of the Democratic Party, which often has difficulty building a consensus within the party, the Republican Party in the House of Representatives in the initial months of the 104th Congress in 1995 was a much more cohesive group. It was quite willing to follow the leadership of its new Speaker to pass the program contained in the House Republicans' campaign manifesto of 1994, the Contract with America. Using Jim Wright's autocratic style as leader of the House from 1987 to 1989 Speaker Gingrich garnered much power and exercised it. However, an attempt to remove him by his party conservatives in the summer of 1997 along with Republican losses in the congressional elections of 1998 led to Gingrich's replacement by Dennis Hastert as Speaker.

Unlike Gingrich, Speaker Hastert worked behind the scenes to increase the power of the Speaker. The Republicans continued to honor the commitment of term limits for committee chairpersons to four Congresses under Hastert's leadership. In addition to this, those interested in a position of chair of a committee had to "interview" with the House leadership. This led to more junior members of a committee passing over more senior members to achieve a committee's leadership position. In 2003 Richard Pombo (R-CA) passed over seven more senior members to win the chairmanship of the House Resources Committee. In 2005, Jerry Lewis (R-CA), competed successfully against Ralph Regula (R-OH) to head the House Appropriations Committee.

When Nancy Pelosi became Speaker in 2007 at the beginning of the 110th Congress, the Democratic party returned to its tradition of honoring seniority on a committee. Thus, John Dingell (D-MI), the oldest and longest serving member of the House, assumed the chairmanship of the powerful Committee on Energy and Commerce. With the election of Barack Obama as president in 2008 and with a larger majority of Democratic members of the House, some Democrats challenged the system with Henry Waxman (D-CA) defeating John Dingell to become the chairman of the House Energy and Commerce Committee for the 111th Congress. This committee produced the House version of the Health Care Reform as well as the Energy, or Climate Change, legislation.

Majority Leader

John Boehner's tenure as Speaker of the House began in January 2011 following the midterm 2010 elections when the Republican party swept the House Democrats from power. As a former committee chairman, Speaker Boehner has allowed the House Republican committee chairmen to take the lead on a conservative legislative agenda. However, even with this more open, relaxed style of leadership, conservative fractions, among them members from the Tea Party movement within the Republican

Conference, have continued to differ with Boehner's negotiations' with the White House on budget matters.

At the beginning of each Congress the majority leader is elected by secret ballot of the majority party's conference, the organization to which all members of a party belong. The last five Democratic Speakers of the House served as majority leader for the Democrats before being elected speaker, demonstrating why this position has been a highly coveted one. Because of the shake-up in the Republican House leadership at the end of 1998 the man ultimately chosen to succeed Gingrich did not hold a leadership position. The majority leader serves as the party's chief floor leader. He or she promotes party votes, assists the Speaker in the timing and setting of the House legislative agenda and serves as a liaison with the White House on the President's legislative program, especially if the President is from the same party. The current majority leader is Eric Cantor (R-VA).

Minority Leader

The House minority leader should have parliamentary and legislative experience in order to lead his colleagues in opposing the legislative measures of the majority party. As titular head of the party the minority leader encourages party unity for a legislative program both in committee and on the House floor.

The minority leader also chairs the chief party organization which makes the committee assignments for members, and also serves as an ex officio member of a party's policy committee, which formulates the party's legislative program. The current minority leader is Nancy Pelosi (D-CA).

whips
The role of the Whip can be traced back to the Parliament of the United Kingdom which adopted the term Whip from the fox-hunting position, 'whipper-in,' or the person who kept the fox hounds focused on their mission.

Majority and Minority Whips

Serving as an assistant to the majority or minority leader the whip constantly works for party discipline and unity behind a legislative program. Assisted by regional whips or zone whips the whip's organizations make head counts for final votes, gather information for the leadership regarding the party's overall attitude on an issue and work to persuade or "whip" the party's membership in line.

The whip organizations are so very much a part of the leadership structure that they are responsible for tracking weekly floor activity. The "whip notice," published by the majority party late on Thursday of each

---

EXERCISE: Senate Leadership in the Constitution
- Go to usconstitution.net
- Click **Single-page** under The United States Constitution; The Text
- Scroll down and Click **Article 1, Section 3 - The Senate**

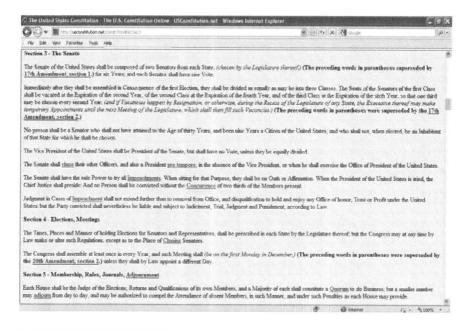

week while the House is in session, contains a list of the legislation to be considered for final passage on the House floor the following week.

The Republican whip is chosen by the Republican Conference, which is composed of all Republican members of the House of Representatives. The Democratic representatives elect the whip in the Democratic Caucus, the Democratic Party organization, at the beginning of each Congress. The current majority House whip is Kevin McCarthy (R-CA) and minority House whip is Steny Hoyer (D-MD).

Leaders in the Senate
President of the Senate

The Constitution provides that the vice president of the United States (in the 112th Congress Joe Biden) serve as the president of the Senate. Presiding rarely over this chamber the vice president does have the power to cast tie-breaking votes, the only vote that he can make in the Senate. With the separation of powers in U.S. government, the position of president of the Senate is the only official participatory role the executive branch has on Capitol Hill (see usconstitution.net, Article I, section 3).

President Pro Tempore

A second Senate officer, the president pro tempore, is called for in the Constitution to preside over the Senate in the absence of the Senate president. This office is third in line, after the vice president and the speaker of the House, to assume the presidency in an emergency. Currently Patrick Leahy (D-VT) holds this position.

Tradition holds that the position of president pro tempore is reserved for the member of the majority party who has served in the Senate for the longest, most continuous period of time. Neither the Senate president nor the president pro tempore has the power and influence as presiding officer that the speaker of the House of Representatives enjoys.

Majority Leader

As the party's floor leader the majority leader is chief strategist for passage of the party's legislative program. The personalized, informal nature of the "Club of 100" (the U.S. Senate) defines this position as one of persuasion, compromise and conciliation. Elected at the beginning of each Congress this Senate leader is responsible for scheduling bills on the floor and serving as liaison with the White House if the President is from the same party. Rules for floor consideration of bills are fewer and less strict than those in the House. Therefore, none of the presiding officers or the majority leader has the power the Speaker of the House has to control debate. Unlike the House Rules Committee, the Senate Rules Committee oversees Senate administrative issues such as office space rather than regulations on amendments and legislation for floor consideration.

Style, experience and personality contribute to a majority leader's success. Leaders such as Howard Baker (R-TN) had the talents and personal touch so necessary to hold together the factions within the party in the early 1980s. Such leadership ability enabled the White House to achieve budget and tax cuts, the Reagan Revolution, in the summer of 1981.

In the last several decades, Democrats have also had successful majority leaders in George Mitchell (D-ME) who achieved passage of amendments to the Clean Air Act in 1990 as a pragmatic and consensus building leader. After the 9/11 attacks Tom Daschle (D-SD), as Democratic majority leader, held his party together to secure passage for the White House's critical national security legislation.

When Dr. Bill Frist (R-TN), experienced both legislative successes as well as failures. Leading the Senate, a body that operates by "unanimous consent" of all its members on any legislative action, requires a leader who constantly works to build agreement among the members of both parties. Knowledge and experience of Senate rules and procedures can make or break a party's (or President's) legislative agenda. Because of the objections through filibuster by the Democrats in 2003 and 2004 to some of President George W. Bush's conservative nominations to federal judicial positions Senator Frist was able to move most, but not all, of the nominations to successful confirmation by the full Senate. Thus, at the beginning of the 109th Congress in 2005, Senator Frist, with the backing of the White House, moved to end the filibuster on judicial nominations. This challenge to the rules and prerogatives of the Senate by Frist led to a bi-partisan effort by senior members of both parties to defeat this initiative to limit the filibuster.

To be sure, Dr. Frist led his party and President to significant legislative successes such as the passage of the Medicare Reform Act in 2003, tax cuts in 2003 and 2004 and the Tort and Bankruptcy Reform legislation in 2005. However, the challenge to his leadership by both Republicans and Democrats described above suggests the difficulties in building "unanimous consent" in the Senate.

Harry Reid (D-NV) has also had difficulty holding the Democratic party together in his years as majority leader from 2007-2010. Conservative senators such as Ben Nelson (D-NB) and Mary Landrieu (D-LA) have opposed measures such as the Stimulus Bill and energy legislation respectively. Such party opposition, in addition to the extensive use of the filibuster by the Republican minority in recent years as previously described, has hindered the operations of the Senate.

In the 112th Congress the Democrats continue to be the majority in the Senate with Harry Reid as Majority Leader with Chuck Schumer (D-NY) assisting in scheduling floor legislation.

Minority Leader

The leader of the minority party in the Senate works for party unity in order to check and to challenge the activities of the majority party. In the event that the President is a member of the same party as the minority leader, the minority leader guides the chief executive's legislative program through the Senate.

The Democratic senators elected Thomas Daschle (D-SD) to serve as their minority leader during the 106th Congress. Daschle, a moderate politician from America's heartland, worked to keep the factions of his party together. Unlike the House where the majority in numbers truly rules, the Senate's rules and procedures may permit the minority to prevail by the use of the filibuster as previously described for President Bush's judicial nominations. In the 112th Congress Mitch McConnell (R-KY) is the Minority Leader.

In the 112th Congress Mitch McConnell (R-KY) served as the Minority Leader for the Republicans in the Senate. His effective use of Senate rules and the filibuster frequently resulted in the minority party in the Senate building roadblocks for passage of legislation. He will continue to serve in this position in the 113th Congress from 2013-2014.

Party Whips

The positions and duties of the whip in the Senate, whether majority or minority, are similar to those of the whip in the House of Representatives. Working for party unity and counting and predicting votes on legislation the majority and minority whips assist their leaders in scheduling legislation for floor consideration and lobbying party colleagues. The whips from the 111th Congress, Dick Durbin (D-IL) and John Cornyn (R-TX) continued in their roles for the 112th Congress, the former as the Majority Whip and the latter as the Minority Whip.

ORGANIZATIONS ON CAPITOL HILL

Now that the leadership positions in both houses of Congress have been described, the organizational side of Capitol Hill deserves attention. The political party organizations of committees and conferences, standing legislative committees and single-issue congressional service organizations comprise the various strata of organizational entities that exist in Congress. Although the leadership endeavors to maintain its control over the legislative activities of its membership, other leaders emerge from each of these strata. This is a reality that suggests just how dispersed power is on Capitol Hill.

Party Organizations on Capitol Hill

In the House of Representatives every Republican is a member of the Republican Conference and every Democrat belongs to the Democratic Caucus. The equivalent organizations in the Senate are called the Republican and Democratic Conferences. These groups elect the party leaders, approve committee assignments, discuss party legislative strategies and policy and sometimes discipline party members by stripping them of their committee assignments.

An example of a party disciplining one of its members is the case of Rep. Phil Gramm, a Democrat from Texas. As a member of the House Budget Committee in 1981 Gramm was privy to the Democrats' plans for opposing the President's budget which he revealed to the Republicans. The Democrats lost all major votes on the budget that summer. On its leadership's recommendation in 1983 the Democratic Party refused to give Gramm his seat on the Budget Committee for the 98th Congress. Very rarely does such reprimanding take place on Capitol Hill. After

Party Organizations on Capitol Hill

House

REPUBLICAN CONFERENCE
- Steering Committee
- Policy Committee
- Campaign Committee

DEMOCRATIC CAUCUS
- Steering Committee
- Policy Committee
- Campaign Committee

Senate

REPUBLICAN CONFERENCE
- Committee on Committees
- Campaign Committee
- Policy Committee

DEMOCRATIC CONFERENCE
- Steering Committee
- Campaign Committee
- Policy Committee

this party disciplinary action, however, Phil Gramm resigned his seat, switched to the Republican Party in 1983 and was reelected to the same seat to serve as a Republican on the Budget Committee. In 1984, he was elected a U.S. Senator from Texas.

The Democrats' ultimate disciplinary action came with the removal of Jim Wright as speaker in 1989.

Under the leadership of Gingrich instances of such disciplinary actions occurred when Mark Neuman (R-WI) temporarily lost his seat on the Appropriations Committee because he had voted against the Republican agenda on some budget issues.

After the 108th Congress that ended in 2004 Republican House leadership moved to punish one of its subcommittee chairman, Chris Smith (R- NJ), who, as leader of the Veterans' Affairs and Related Agencies Subcommittee, had refused to raise the funding for NASA for fiscal year 2005 (NASA is located in then Majority Leader Tom Delay's Texas district).

Senate Republicans

Republican Committee on Committees
Membership
• Preferred senators and senior members
Task: Determine all committee assignments

Republican Policy Committee
Membership
• Preferred senators and senior members
Task: Research, coordinate and unify party's legislative agenda

National Republican Senatorial Committee
Membership
• Preferred senators and senior members
Task: Aid both new candidates and incumbents in elections

Senate Democrats

Democratic Steering Committee
Membership
• Party Leadership
• Senior senators
Task: Determine all committee assignments

Democratic Policy Committee
Membership
• Preferred senators and senior members
Task: Recommend positions for the party to take on legislation

Democratic Senator Campaign Committee
Membership
• Preferred senators and senior members
Task: Support the election of new senators and the re-election of incumbents

House Republicans

Republican Steering Committee

Membership
- Party's selected leaders
- Members from various geographical areas
- Representatives from freshman and sophomore classes

Task: Determine all committee assignments

Republican Policy Committee

Membership
- Nearly 50 members of the House

Tasks
- Unite the party
- Set party policy and strategy

National Republican Congressional Committee

Tasks
- Assist the campaigns of House candidates
- Support the re-election of incumbents

House Democrats

Democratic Steering & Policy Committee

Membership
- 45 members including:
  - Party leaders
  - Members from various geographic areas
  - Senior members on House Appropriations and Ways & Means Committees

Task: Determine all committee assignments

Democratic Policy Committee

Membership
- Nearly 50 members of the House

Tasks
- Assists the Democratic Caucus' and the party's policy agenda
- Sets legislative priorities

Democratic Congressional Campaign Committee

Tasks
- Assist the campaigns of House candidates
- Support the re-election of incumbents

At the beginning of the 109th Congress, Rep. Smith was thrown off the Appropriations Committee and his subcommittee was abolished.

When the Democrats controlled the House of Representatives from 2007-2010, Speaker Pelosi and her party's caucus forced the retirement from Congress of Eric Massa (D-NY) because of his questionable behavior toward male members of his staff. When William Jefferson (D-LA) was found with $90,000 cash in his office refrigerator, the House leadership forced his resignation from the House Ways and Means Committee. And finally, Sander Levin (D-MI) succeeded Charles Rangel (D-NY) as chairman of the powerful House Ways and Means Committee when Rangel was the subject of investigation for tax evasion on some rental property.

There are another dozen or so party groups in the House and the Senate. The functions and names of the most important ones follow.

COMMITTEE ORGANIZATIONS

Most of the substantive work of drafting legislation takes place in committee on Capitol Hill. Because of this the role and power of committee and subcommittee chairpersons of the more than 200 committees on the Hill have grown in recent years. In fact, "government by subcommittee" has described the power source scheme in Congress since the late 1970s. If a subcommittee chairperson refuses to hold a hearing on a piece of legislation, there is little, if anything, the party leadership can do. Although viewed by many as a subversion of the power of the leadership and the more senior committee chairpersons, the scattering of power represents, perhaps, a Congress that is more open to and more influenced by outside forces, whether they are constituents, lobbyists or political action committees.

Because of the nature of Senate rules, or lack thereof, and because of its more collegial tone traditionally, senators have tried to work together to pass legislation through committee. However, with the election of Barack Obama as president in 2008 which also resulted in a greater majority of senate Democrats, the Republican party, led by Mitch McConnell (R-KY), held fast in opposing the White House and the Democrats' legislative agendas. With the exception of the Recovery or Stimulus Act passed in 2009 when three Republicans voted with the Democrats for the bill's final passage, Republicans, even in committee, opposed important legislation such as climate change, health care and financial institution reform.

When the Republicans took charge of the House of Representatives for the first time in 40 years in 1995, rules changes were made in an effort to limit the power of the committee and subcommittee chairpersons. The term of a chairperson was limited to six years or three congresses. In addition to this change legislation referred to a full committee would not necessarily have to be referred to subcommittee for consideration.

As was stated above, the committee chairpersons became more independent of the Republican House leadership after the 105th Congress. Such independence began with John Kasich, chair of the Budget Committee, who refused to write a budget resolution in 1998 because of differences over the size of tax cuts he wanted. Richard Pombo (R-CA), as chairman of the House Resources Committee in the 108th and 109th Congresses, refused to allow subcommittee consideration of the reauthorization of the Endangered Species Act. Don Young (R-AK), Alaska's sole representative, as chair of the Transportation and Infrastructure Committee, oversaw the passage of the largest amount of money for local highway projects in history in 2005 (P.L. 109-59[See following Exercise]). The bill exceeded the caps on which the White House and the party leadership had agreed. Describing the special projects for members (There were more than 6,000!), Young said of the legislation, "We stuffed it like a turkey." (Note: In 1987, President Ronald Reagan vetoed a highway bill that had 157 projects.)

During the 111th Congress, from 2009-2010, the House Democratic leadership controlled much of the legislation that was considered and passed by the committees. As was previously mentioned, with the demise of the conference committee, the House majority leadership retained power in an effort to manage better and control the flow of legislation. No John Kasich or Richard Pombo or Don Young defied the direction of Speaker Pelosi during the 111th Congress.

CONGRESSIONAL MEMBER ORGANIZATIONS

Congressional Member Organizations (CMOs) are informal organizations of members of the House of Representatives who join together to share official resources in pursuit of common legislative and research objectives. Funding for such organizations derives from a member's personal staff account and other resources under the member's control

"Inside the Beltway"
A phrase used to characterize parts of the real or imagined American political system. It refers to the Capital Beltway (Interstate 495), that encircles Washington D.C.

EXERCISE: P.L. 109-59
- Go to thomas.gov
- Under More Legislation click Public Laws
- Under Select Congress click 109
- Under Select a Range of Public Laws click 109-1 - 109-150
- Scroll down to 59.
- Go down to final line: Latest Major Action: Became Public Law No: 109-59 [GPO: Text, PDF].
- Click on either Text of PDF
- You will now be directed to the GPO (Government Printing Office). Click Continue to GPO Site.
- The text of the Public Law will be displayed.

These organizations have no separate offices on Capitol Hill and may not use the frank or a member's frank (mailing) privilege. Issue caucuses still exist in the Senate, but the most active and vociferous are at work in the House.

Currently, there are more than 400 CMOs in the House including the Congressional Aviation and Space Caucus, Caucus on Community Health Care Centers, the Climate Change Caucus, the Pro-Life Caucus, the Steel Caucus, and the Taiwan Caucus to name a few. The Senate has fewer of these organizations, only about 100, that range from the Senate Beef Caucus to the Rural Health Caucus to the Western Senate Coalition. Interestingly enough, there are nearly 50 bi-cameral CMOs, such as the Asian Pacific American Caucus, the Black Caucus, the Hispanic Caucus, the Internet Caucus, the Soybean Caucus and the Vietnam Era Veterans in Congress Caucus.

SUMMARY

One of the difficult aspects of Congress for an outsider to understand is the dispersal of power and absence of party authority on Capitol Hill. Unlike the other democratically elected legislative bodies that are also parliamentary forms of government, the Congress of the United States is a representative legislature, a legislature that responds to the interests of voters and not primarily to those of party ideology.

Obviously, the impeachment proceedings against President Clinton by the 105th Congress were indeed partisan both in consideration and in the final vote by the full House on the two articles to impeach the President and the votes in the Senate that failed to convict him. However, some scholars who have studied Congress since World War II have shown by analysis of votes in the House and the Senate that partisanship on Capitol Hill has never been great. On the other hand public perception these days is that there is more partisanship "inside the Beltway" among the Members of Congress than among the American people. Certainly the midterm election results of 2010 suggest otherwise with the emergence on the Tea Party movement within the Republican party and an American electorate unhappy about the country's economic situation.

NOTES

COMMITTEES ON CAPITOL HILL

Most of the major work of lawmaking in the U.S. Congress takes place in the committees and subcommittees of the U.S. Senate and the House of Representatives. More than 100 years ago Woodrow Wilson wrote, "It is not far from the truth to say that Congress in session is Congress on public exhibition, whilst Congress in its committee rooms is Congress at work." To appreciate better the workings of Capitol Hill an understanding of the committee system is vital.

With over 10,000 pieces of legislation introduced in each Congress, a filtering mechanism must exist to produce the best possible laws. The committees in the House and the Senate provide the needed review function that ultimately results in fewer than 600 bills being signed into law every two years. These "work groups" draft and craft legislation. The committee process is central to the deliberative path of legislation through both the House and the Senate.

Until the early 1970s the power of the committees rested with the chairpersons, many of whom had served for more than 20 years in the Senate and 30 years in the House of Representatives. The Democratic majority in the House and the Senate in the 1950s and

1960s meant that its party members could serve as chairpersons of the committees. This "seniority system," as it was called then, closed off the opportunity for younger members of Congress to advance to positions of importance in committee. Before 1973, most committees did not have subcommittees, which suggests that the power of a committee rested totally with the chairperson. Men such as Tom Connelly and Clarence Cannon in the Senate and Wilbur Mills and Wright Patman in the House ruled their committees with an iron hand for many years.

When the younger generation, the so-called "Watergate babies," entered Congress in the early 1970s, they demanded greater participation in the committee system. Through rules changes in the House and the Senate they succeeded in establishing a more open committee system in terms of membership and work activity. This "victory" by the younger members led to a growth in the number of subcommittees from 1975 to 1995. This made the legislative process all the more complex and confusing to the outsider. With slightly more than 200 committees and subcommittees holding hearings on Capitol Hill the task of following a piece of legislation became a challenge although not an impossible one.

When the Republicans won control of the House after the elections of 1994, many of their rules changes included a reduction in the number of committees and subcommittees. In an attempt to cut down on jurisdictional overlap and to save money the House abolished three full committees and 20 subcommittees at the beginning of the 104th Congress in 1995. The Senate did not abolish any committees or subcommittees at that time.

Since 2001, with the exception of the House and Senate Appropriations Committees and the House Homeland Security Committee, the number of committees and subcommittees in the House and the Senate has remained the same.

Exercise: House and Senate Committees

Go to **house.gov.**

Click on the **arrow** to the right of the second drop down box.

All of the House Committees appear.

Go to **senate.gov.**

Click on the **HEARINGS** button on the menu bar.

The Senate Committees are listed in red.

TYPES OF COMMITTEES

While the lawmaking committees, referred to as the standing committees and found on the house.gov and senate.gov homepages, are the most active groups, there are also study committees, select committees, joint committees and conference committees.

Standing Committees

In the last 15 years the names of some of the House authorization committees have changed. The House Armed Services Committee, so called for 40 years when the Democrats controlled the House of

Committees in Congress

Standing Committees

Permanent legislative committees

AUTHORIZATION
Committees that draft laws to create programs

APPROPRIATIONS
Committees that fund programs

Study Committees

Nonpermanent special issue committees

SELECT
Committees that may be formed in each chamber to study special issues

JOINT
Combined House and Senate special issue committees

Conference Committees

Ad hoc committees of House and Senate members formed to reach consensus on legislative language in a bill that requires final agreement by both the full House and Senate

Representatives, was changed to the Committee on National Security when the Republicans first took control of the House following the 1994 midterm elections. In 1999 the House decided to give this military affairs committee its old name, the House Armed Services Committee. The House Banking Committee became the Financial Services Committee in 1995 and has retained this title even when the Democrats took control of the House in 2007.

No matter which party has controlled the Senate in the last 15 years, the names of the full committees have remained the same with a few minor changes in the names of some of the subcommittees.

There are 36 standing committees in the Congress - 16 in the Senate and 20 in the House. Covering a broad range of issue areas that touch all aspects of American life from agriculture to taxes to highways to health care to MX missiles to international trade to homeland security these committees draft and amend the legislation referred to them by the parliamentarians in each house.

Each of these committees has several subcommittees. The Appropriations Committees (the money committees in each body) have the largest number of subcommittees (12 in the Senate and 12 in the House). In the House, each committee has an average of five subcommittees. The Senate sets no limits on the number of subcommittees. There may be as few as four or as many as seven subcommittees.

Two categories of standing committees exist in both the House and the Senate. The authorizing committees are the programmatic committees and subcommittees that draft laws to create federally funded programs such as student loans, Medicare and nuclear submarines. However, just because a program has been created does not mean that the money will be available for the execution of it. The power to fund programs rests in the Appropriations Committees in the House and the

Senate.

As mentioned above, each of these Appropriations Committees has subcommittees whose powerful chairpersons and membership determine how many dollars will be spent for each program. For example, the Senate Energy and Natural Resources may authorize $800 million for the restoration of fire-ravaged national forest lands while the Interior Subcommittee on Appropriations may have planned for only $450 million or, perhaps, had decided not to fund any program at all. To complete a possible scenario the House of Representatives may have appropriated $300 million. Since the legislative language must be the same in both houses for a law to be enacted, the differences must be resolved in a final conference.

While money bills receive consideration by committees each year, most legislation sent to committee dies there, never having received a hearing.

If a bill receives any consideration at all, the subcommittee of a full committee with specific jurisdiction normally holds the first hearing. For example, if a bill on a program to build F-18 fighter planes is introduced in the House of Representatives, it is sent to the House Armed Services Committee whose chairperson then refers it to the Subcommittee on Air and Land Forces where hearings may take place. In the "mark-up" process changes may be made to a bill. When these changes are incorporated into the bill, a "clean" bill is then sent to the full committee for consideration.

A bill may receive a favorable vote in subcommittee, but it still may not be considered by the full committee. If a chairperson does not favor a piece of legislation, he or she can refuse to hold hearings on a bill for many months or not at all. Throughout the 1980s John Dingell (D-MI), Chairperson of the House Energy and Commerce Committee, delayed hearings or refused to hold hearings on clean air legislation and killed

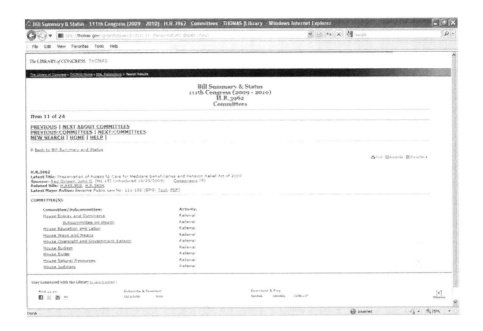

the measure in committee. When the Republicans controlled Congress from 2001-2006 during the first six years of George W. Bush's presidency, no Republican committee or subcommittee chairman held hearings on climate change despite the emerging scientific information concerning the issue. The Bush White House was not interested in supporting any legislation; some Republican chairmen in Congress dismissed the issue of climate change as a "myth."

The progress of a legislative proposal outlined above occurs if a bill is tightly drafted. That is to say it covers only one issue area. If a bill is broadly drafted, it may receive multiple, split or sequential referral to committee. Joint referral means that the bill is sent to several committees for consideration. Sequential referral means that the bill must be considered first by one committee and then, following that consideration, by other committees. Split referral means that parts of the bill are to be considered by various committees.

Exercise: House Appropriations Committee

Go to **house.gov.**

Click on the **arrow** to the right of the second drop down box.

All of the House Committees appear.

Click on **Appropriations**, then click **GO** to the right of the drop down box.

Click on the **SUBCOMMITTEES** button on the menu bar.

Links to all of the Subcommittees can be found on the left with information about each Subcommittee Office in the middle of the page.

Visit Committee websites in both the House and Senate which you have an interest in. Explore their Subcommittees to see the members and their jurisdiction. You will notice that every committee website is set up differently so it may take some "hunting and clicking" to navigate these sites.

Let us take the case of split referral for purposes of discussion, the H.R. 3962 Preservation of Access to Care for Medicare Beneficiaries and Pension Relief Act of 2010. Initial consideration of this bill began in the House of Representatives by means of a split referral. Because of the market-driven nature of America's health care system the business portion of the bill was initially referred to the Committee on Energy and Commerce and then to its Subcommittee on Health. The bill also addressed Medicare that is paid for mainly through payroll taxes. Thus, that portion of the bill was referred to the Committee on Ways and Means, the House tax committee and its Subcommittee on Health. Since President Barack Obama had promised legislation on health care during his campaign for president and with Congress controlled by the Democrats, the health care legislation had the political impetus to move to final passage.

However, split referral may make consideration and passage of a bill longer, if impossible, if it covers a broad range of issue areas. If one part of a bill with four parts or titles involves taxes, rules would require that the Ways and Means Committee in the House and the Finance Committee in the Senate consider the section on revenues or taxes. It is possible that the other three parts of the bill may be referred to three other committees such as Banking, Commerce and Public Works.

Select Committees

Select or special committees in both the Senate and the House study issues affecting a very specific area. Several of these committees, such as the Senate Select Committee on Aging and the Permanent Select Committee on Intelligence, have become more permanent in nature. Technically established for two years, they offer recommendations for legislation.

The hearings of these committees provide forums where the elderly may appear before a committee to make a public statement on the status and problems of the constituents for whom they speak. Often legislation is introduced because of the recommendations that are made by these committees.

In an effort to streamline the work of Congress the House changed its rules in 1995 to limit its members' service to two on standing committees and to four on subcommittees. There is no such rule in the Senate.

Joint Committees

Joint committees, consisting of an equal number of senators and representatives, hold hearings that result in policy recommendations in the areas of economics and tax. Generally speaking the Library, Economic, Printing and Taxation joint committees do not draft laws but rather provide in-depth studies for the direction of future legislation.

Conference Committees - *Formerly*

A final type of committee on Capitol Hill is the conference committee, or "final board of review" of legislation before it is passed. This committee is formed when a piece of legislation, whether a bill or a joint or concurrent resolution, has passed both the Senate and the House but with different language. Since legislation must pass both the House and the Senate in identical form, differences between the House and Senate versions are resolved "in conference." Until 1975 these conference sessions were closed to the public. However, rules changes in both the Senate and the House opened these meetings to the public. It should be noted that even though the sessions are technically open at the conference stage, the rooms for the conference sessions are often quite small and seating is limited. In recent years conference committees have been closed.

The size and membership of this committee, under the rules, are determined by the leadership of both houses. But in practice, the chairperson and the ranking minority member of a committee involved appoint the representatives and the senators. When a final vote is taken by the conference committee, the committee dissolves.

It should be noted here that these groups are quite important to the legislative process. If either the House or the Senate rejects the report of a conference on a piece of legislation, the bill or resolution will fail to clear the remaining legislative hurdles.

Conference Committees - *Currently*

The changing nature of the conference has already been discussed at length in Chapter 1. Even with the loss of seats in the House as a result of the 2012 elections, the republicans still control this chamber where limited or exclusive membership on these committees may continue.

SUMMARY

The committee system, so crucial to the lawmaking process on Capitol Hill, reflects the deliberative nature of Congress. With deliberation often comes tension, which can slow the progress of a bill through the legislative channels. Such seemingly excessive examination appears to be uncalled for as well as inefficient. However, another way of looking at this "poor way of doing business" is to realize that Congress, the representative body that it is, reflects the complexities of twentieth-first century American society whose fabric is woven so tightly that issue areas of public policy are often closely related to one another.

NOTES

COMMITTEES AND THE HEARING PROCESS

4

There is no greater example of the dual roles of representative and lawmaker than the activities of senators and representatives in committee. Most of the drafting of legislation takes place in committee. Very closely tied to this lawmaking responsibility are the realities of being an elected representative which often affects the makeup and workload of a committee, as well as the nature of the hearings themselves.

MEMBERSHIP ON A COMMITTEE

In November of each election year all 441 (including the six delegates from territories) seats in the House and one-third of the Senate seats are contested for election. In the House newly elected members will be assigned to their first committees and returning members can seek reassignment on the same or other committees. Although fewer changes should occur in the Senate, since fewer seats are open for election, committee assignment or reassignment can be a major task among the "Club of 100." Throughout the 1980s there were more changes than usual as the Senate changed from a Democratic to a Republican majority in 1980 and as the Democrats regained control in 1986.

With the congressional elections of 1994 all committee and subcommittee chairpersons in both the House and the Senate changed because the Republicans, with majorities in both chambers, took control of the legislative branch of government. The 2010 midterm elections resulted in Republican control of the House which means that the control the committees and subcommittees in the 112th Congress will be under Republican control. As was previously mentioned, House rules have limited the tenure of all chairpersons of full committees and subcommittees to three congresses, or six years. Also, membership on House committees is limited to no more than two full committees and four subcommittees. At the beginning of the 106th Congress in 1999 the Senate also passed a rule to limit the term on committee chairpersons to six years. There is no limit on committee assignments in the Senate.

The leadership organization of each party in the Senate and the House determines committee assignments. The party with the majority of seats in each chamber will assign the committee chairpersons and the majority/minority ratio of committee membership.

When the election is over, another kind of campaign begins - that of the members of Congress to gain seats on the committees of their choice. With an eye toward reelection, especially in the House, members seek assignments to committees with issues having the greatest effect on their district or state. Although the committee is the forum for lawmaking, the representative nature of the Congress comes through when the composition of the committee's membership is examined. Generally, the older members, who know one another and the leadership, fare better in desired committee assignments than the freshmen. However, effective lobbying of the leadership and party colleagues between the election and the new Congress in January can pay off even for new members. It is possible for a new congressman to be on a powerful money committee if he or she has the support of senior members.

When the Republicans gained control of the House in 1994, Speaker Newt Gingrich made sure that several of the 73 freshmen class received plum assignments to the powerful Ways and Means and Appropriations Committees, passing over more senior members in the Republican Party. In the 112th Congress beginning in 2011 the new Speaker of the House, John Boehner (R-OH), may assign freshmen members to these important committees.

Even the more senior members of Congress keep the people back home in mind. Joe Barton (R-TX), who has represented Texas' Sixth District for 26 years, chaired the Committee on Energy and Commerce from 2003-2006. Having served on this committee for most of his time in Congress, he appreciates and protects the energy interests of the state of Texas.

Senate leadership also considers a state's interests when committee assignments are made. Many seats on the Energy and Natural Resources Committee are held by senators from the West, where most of the public lands are located. The appointments of John Barrasso (R-WY) and Jeff Bingaman (D-NM) are good examples.

This desire to represent a state or district's interests should not be interpreted as totally undermining the policymaking process of Congress. In fact, some committee chairpersons have come from areas of the country that are not directly affected by the issues that they spend hours, days and even years deliberating. Lee Hamilton (D-IN) was an individual who - having a safe seat - worked in areas more international in nature for several years. He was the ranking minority member of the House International Relations Committee before his retirement from Congress in 1998. Alan Simpson who represented Wyoming for three terms worked tirelessly on immigration issues.

Some recent committee assignments in the Senate reflect national issues that concern all of American society. Beginning with the 1992 elections, more women were elected to the Senate than ever before, bringing the total number to 14 female senators in 2005, five Republicans and nine Democrats. Many of these women campaigned on platforms for women's issues such as increased funding for breast cancer research and more equality in the work place. In the most recently concluded 111th Congress, Diane Feinstein (D-CA) and Amy Klobuchar (D-MN) served on the Senate Judiciary Committee, the formerly all-white, male panel. At the beginning of the 112th Congress in January of 2011 there were 17 female senators, 12 Democrats and five Republicans.

Indeed, a seat on a powerful, prestigious committee in Congress could mean greater influence and media attention to a representative and especially to a senator. Over the years the stature of committees has changed according to America's interests, international involvement and needs.

Prestigious Committees

In the wake of the terrorist attacks on the U.S. on September 11, 2001 and war in Iraq, the Armed Services and International Affairs Committees regained their prestige.

With the recent financial difficulties and government cutbacks, assignment to the Appropriations Committee (approving funds for federal projects) is not considered a prestigious assignment.

In recent years on Capitol Hill the tax, budget and money committees as well as the energy and armed services committees have been among the more powerful and prestigious. During the early 1970s the Senate Foreign Relations and House Foreign Affairs committees and judiciary committees held national prominence because of Vietnam and Watergate, and membership on these committees was coveted. With the end of the Cold War in the early 1990s and the controversy over social agenda issues such as school prayer and abortion in the 1980s few people willingly wanted to serve as members on the Judiciary and International Affairs committees. Congress has also established the Committees on Homeland Security in an effort to oversee the federal government's initiatives to shore up the safety of Americans on the home front.

Also, with the rise of the conservative right's political influence and power, conservative members again covet positions on the Judiciary Committee in both houses of Congress to push the social conservative agenda.

Over time the House Committee on Energy and Commerce and the Senate Committee on Energy and Natural Resources have become powerful and prestigious committees on which to hold seats. The oil crisis of the 1970s and President Carter's effort to draft an energy legislation package, concern about government deregulation in the 1980s, the growing environmental movement, the nation's growing dependence on foreign oil and the emergence of the climate change issue have contributed to the greater prominence of these committees today.

TYPES OF COMMITTEE HEARINGS

Four types of committee hearings take place in Congress. Legislative, oversight, and investigation hearings are held in both the Senate and the House while the Constitution calls for confirmation hearings to occur only in the Senate. The location, tone and timing of these congressional hearings do not evolve in a vacuum. Much of the content of hearings on Capitol Hill has to do with the agenda of a committee's chairperson and his or her committee staff who are responding to the country's legislative needs, the interests of the people back home and the lobbying groups in Washington.

Exercise: Hearing Schedule

Go to woodsinstitute.com.

On the left side of the page are Links to Your Government.

Click on **U.S. House of Representatives Activity**. This navigates you to the Office of the Clerk of the House. This page lists floor proceedings and other events that affect the entire house.

Return to **woodsinstitute.com**

Click on **Today's House Committee Hearings**. This takes you to Radio-Television Correspondents Gallery. After 3 pm each day, this site lists the Committee Hearings for the following day.

Return to **woodsinstitute.com.**

Click on the **U.S. Senate Activity** link. This navigates to a site that lists Senate proceedings on the floor and other Senate activity.

For a Senate Hearing Schedule return to **woodsinstitute.com** and click **Today's Senate Committee Hearings**. The Senate maintains its own site for hearings and is updated weekly.

Many people complain that hearings are totally orchestrated and often exist merely to provide photo opportunities for members on the nightly news. To a certain extent this is true since the chairperson and committee staff schedule the time and place of the hearings. Depending on the issue these public hearings (i.e., legislative, oversight, and investigative) may even be held in a representative's home district or senator's state as well as on Capitol Hill. (Hearings that take place outside of Washington are referred to as field hearings.)

Legislative Hearings

The most common hearings are those that consider bills to change existing law. Creation of new federal programs and amendments to or elimination of existing ones takes place in legislative hearings. Because of the importance of these lawmaking committees the discussion of their proceedings will be more involved than that for the oversight, investigative and confirmation hearings.

Not every bill that is introduced receives a hearing. In fact, most do not and die in committee. Generating interest in a bill presents one of the greatest challenges to a bill's sponsor. This is especially true if the legislation is local in nature that is affecting only his or her district or state.

Hearings on Capitol Hill

Legislative Hearings

Review of specific bills

Oversight Hearings

Ongoing review of established programs

Investigation Hearings

Pursuit of suspected illegal activities

Confirmation Hearings

Senate review of high-level presidential appointees

Just as lobbying fellow colleagues for a seat on a particular committee offers a means to a desired end, so will a member successfully obtain a hearing on his or her bill through constant communication with the membership. Obviously, membership on the committee to which one's bill is referred helps, especially if the chairperson expresses an interest in the legislation. Also, circulation of a "Dear Colleague" letter to the 440 other House or 99 Senate offices in an effort to find cosponsors will publicize and promote the legislation. Press conferences help, too. At the beginning of the 104th Congress legislation to implement the provisions in the House Republicans' election manifesto, the Contract with America, received immediate hearings by committees in the House of Representatives. The promise to vote on all measures in the contract during the first 100 days of the 104th Congress was taken seriously by the new chairpersons. Media and general interest by the public helped push this agenda forward.

One more interesting way to obtain a hearing is by involving the executive branch, which in the twentieth century greatly influenced the legislative agenda on the Hill. The influence and power exerted from the White House can be the best way to ensure that a hearing will or will not occur. Thus, when Barack Obama became president in 2009 with large Democratic majorities in both the House and the Senate, there was a great deal of momentum to promote and pass his legislative agenda. In the face of the worst economic crisis since the 1930s the Recovery or stimulus package passed in February of 2009 with the help of three Republican senators. Health care reform, financial institution reform, equal pay for women, the child health care program, twice vetoed by President George W. Bush, and tax cuts were among the many bills that were signed in to law. But the economy continued to stall with unemployment at nearly 10%. November 2, 2010 proved to be a disastrous election day for the

Democrats who lost 63 seats in the House and six in the Senate.

Of course, crisis can push the legislative agenda forward as well. After the 9/11 attacks in 2001, in a matter of a few weeks with very little deliberation, committee consideration or negotiation, Congress passed and the President signed into law legislation such as the Patriot Act, the Airline Bailout Act and the Transportation Security Act. The disastrous hurricane seasons of 2004 and 2005 also brought immediate congressional action for passage of supplemental spending bills for relief for tens of thousands of Americans.

If a chairperson agrees to hold a hearing, he and his staff draw up a list of witnesses to appear before the committee. Witnesses who favor or oppose the legislation can come from any number of sources. Individuals with a certain area of expertise or reputation, such as Henry Kissinger, a former secretary of state, are invited to appear alone. For the most part, however, panels of three or four witnesses with similar views testify together.

In the case of the impact of new immigration policy elected state, local, and county officials testified as a group on Capitol Hill. If the issue is environmental in nature, representatives from the Fish and Wildlife Federation, Friends of the Earth and the Wilderness Society may form a panel. A five-minute summary of the testimony is usually read at the time of the hearing. Members of the committee then are each given a certain amount of time to question the witnesses. Usually, the more senior members of the majority party begin the questioning.

Since most of the committee work on Capitol Hill takes place on Tuesday, Wednesday and Thursday, the committee staff makes sure that the "best" witnesses appear early in the week or even early in a session of Congress. The consideration of proposed amendments to the Constitution in the area of social policy (e.g., prayer in the schools, busing and anti-abortion) during the early 1980s provides an example of the chairperson's power. Peter Rodino (D-NJ), then chairperson of the House Judiciary Committee, opposed these proposed amendments. He proceeded to hold hearings on these amendments and invited hundreds of witnesses to testify before the committee over a period of 14 months without ever calling for a vote. This power of scheduling by a chairperson illustrates well where much authority is held on Capitol Hill. In contrast to the Democrats the Republican-controlled Judiciary Committee in the House in the last decade held numerous hearings and voted out many constitutional amendments and bills backing the conservative right's social agenda. On the other hand when Rep. Richard Pombo chaired the House Resources Committee in the early 2000s, he held months of hearings on the reauthorization of the Endangered Species Act (which he opposed) and never called for a markup or a vote.

Frequently, witnesses and citizens are disappointed when only one or two members of a committee are present to listen to testimony. However, the testimony itself, which must be submitted to the committee at least 24 hours in advance of the hearing, is read by the staff and sometimes by the members and is included in the committee transcript. Since so much information is given out in advance and because of demanding schedules, members of a committee often do not feel compelled to attend a hearing. However, if the press and television news cameras are scheduled to cover a hearing, attendance is usually quite high.

Under the House rules the presence of two members of a committee or a subcommittee constitutes a quorum in order to hold congressional hearings and gather testimony. Depending on a committee's rules one-third of the committee must be present to take up amendments and other business. To report a bill out of committee a majority of the members must be present. In the Senate, where currently nearly every Democratic Senator chairs at least one committee or subcommittee, only one member of the majority party must be present for a hearing to be held.

After the public hearings have been completed, the public markup takes place. It is at this time that changes in the legislation are made. Committee members along with the committee's staff review the bill title by title, line by line and word for word. Members who wish to offer amendments do so. They cast their votes for or against the proposed changes being very much aware of the presence of lobbying groups, executive branch personnel and some citizenry. These markup sessions are where the interest groups and the administration find committee members who are willing to sponsor amendments that will promote their causes.

Under the rules of the House of Representatives proxy voting no longer takes place in committee or subcommittee. In addition, all votes on bills and amendments in committee will be published, and all hearings will be open to the public. Finally, the procedure of a "rolling quorum" - holding open a committee vote indefinitely - that had been practiced by the Democrats has also been eliminated.

Rarely are these amendments overturned by the committee or on the House or Senate floor. Complaints of too much congressional power abiding in subcommittee have some validity. Powerful interest groups with the dollars and technology to generate huge mailings from voters in a member's district or home state have greatly affected the

environment on the Hill and the way business is conducted. The combination of an effective lobbying contact in Washington with a sense of the political pulse of the state and district has had a tremendous effect on the U.S. Congress, an institution still sensitive to the voters back home.

If the full committee considers a piece of legislation and votes to accept it, the staff then prepares a committee report to accompany the bill. The report is very important for it serves to a great extent as the bill's legislative history and provides guidance to those who will be responsible for implementing its terms. It is also the document that most members read rather than reading the legislation. Finally, it must accompany the bill for floor consideration.

This last requirement is often used by a chairperson who opposes a bill that was voted favorably out of his or her committee. Staff can be ordered to take months to write the report. This tactic could effectively kill the bill, since Congress may adjourn before a vote on the bill is taken.

Oversight Hearings

Nowhere is the evidence more obvious that Congress is reviewer and deliberator than in the exercise of its oversight function in committees. As the legislative branch Congress makes laws while the executive branch implements them. As the funding source of programmatic legislation Congress feels that it has the right to review or investigate the activities of departments and agencies in the executive branch.

The activities of the Committee on Homeland Security, the Governmental Affairs Committee in the Senate and the Committee on Government Reform and Oversight in the House concentrate on investigating areas of waste and inefficiency that may exist in federal agencies. The authorization for funding the Government Accountability

Office, the investigative "watch dog" of the Congress, comes from these committees. There are also subcommittees, such as the Subcommittee on the Internal Revenue Service of the Senate Finance Committee and the subcommittees on oversight and investigation of several House committees, whose work is primarily that of review, oversight and investigation. Furthermore, all standing committees on Capitol Hill have oversight responsibilities. Authorizing committees have the power to "deauthorize" federal programs if on review they are found unsuccessful or inefficient. Appropriations committees can refuse to refund programs, thereby making them unable to operate.

In recent years hurricane catastrophes, especially that of Katrina in 2005, moved Congress to conduct oversight hearings on the organization and activity of the Federal Emergency Management Agency (FEMA). As the 112th Congress begins with the Republicans in control of the House, there may well be oversight hearings on the activities of the Obama Administration. A good example would be the expenditures of the Recovery Act money, how much and where.

Investigation Hearings

Oversight hearings often can lead to investigative reviews. In fact, the line between these two activities is quite fine. Investigation hearings take place when a review of an agency's activities suggests that something illegal has taken place. Such hearings increased in the 1980s mostly because of the growth of federal laws and regulations, which affect voters more than ever, and huge budget deficits, which led to greater scrutiny of federal programs.

Congressional review of the Iran-Contra affair during the 100th Congress best illustrates investigative hearings. Although a joint committee of Senators and Representatives conducted the Iran-Contra investigation, there have been instances when several committees have pursued an agenda because of a questionable issue. For example, as many as six committees in the House called special hearings in 1983 at which the Environmental Protection Agency's administrator, Ann Burford Gorsuch, appeared and was "grilled." These probings resulted in her resignation and the conviction and jailing of her deputy, Rita Lavelle, who oversaw the Superfund. Committees in the 101st Congress called for extensive investigation of the Federal Savings and Loan Insurance Corporation in the wake of the catastrophic failures of savings and loan companies across the country. The 103rd Congress held several hearings on the Whitewater affair involving President Clinton and his wife.

In the 105th Congress the Senate and House Government Committees conducted investigative hearings on the issue of campaign fundraising for Clinton's re-election campaign in 1996. Sen. Fred Thompson (R-TN), the chairman of the Senate Government Affairs Committee, and Rep. Dan Burton (R-IN), the chairman of the House Government Reform and Oversight Committee held months of hearings and spent millions of dollars investigating the possible impropriety of the Clinton-Gore 1996 re-election committee to determine if any illegal actions warranted criminal prosecution. Neither committee found substantive evidence to proceed with an indictment.

Since 2001, there have been little to no major investigations conducted by Congress. Even with the 9/11 attacks, the questions about intelligence on weapons of mass destruction prior to the war with Iraq, the enormous no-bid contracts given to Halliburton Industries and others, government investigation of these matters, if at all, has been conducted by commissions or special prosecutors not by the U.S. Congress.

Confirmation Hearings

Only the Senate holds confirmation hearings. Serving as a kind of "ad hoc" oversight function the panels seek to review the past activities of future cabinet secretaries, ambassadors, federal judges and Supreme Court justices who have been nominated by the President. Some of these hearings go smoothly as in the case of Condolezza Rice's nomination and confirmation as Secretary of State at the beginning of the 109th Congress. With the death of William Rehnquist, Chief Justice of the Supreme Court in the summer of 2005, the Senate also confirmed with little opposition his successor, John Roberts.

Senate confirmation of judicial nominations has not always occurred easily in recent years. In the early years of the George W. Bush's presidency (2001-2004) Democrats in the Senate, led by the Minority Leader Tom Daschle (D-SD), opposed nominations of conservatives to the federal bench with the filibuster. Some, but not all of these nominations, have succeeded. And, finally, when in 2005 President Bush proposed his Chief White House Counsel, Harriet Miers, to succeed retiring Sandra Day O'Conner, the conservative intellectual and religious right so opposed her nomination that she never received hearings in the Senate Judiciary Committee and her nomination was withdrawn. The Senate in the 112th Congress (2011) changed the rule to eliminate the "secret" hold on nominations.

SUMMARY

Some people argue that the hearing process is so well orchestrated that not much takes place in a useful, substantive way. However, it is important to remember that these hearings do occur, and they are open to the public. America has a representative and not a parliamentary government. Superseding the political party agenda are the interests of constituents and the lobbying groups that represent many of them. These interests are of chief concern to members of Congress when they serve on committees.

Exercise: Hearing Witness List

Go to **house.gov**

Select **Committee on Energy and Commerce** from the drop down list and click **Go**.

Click **Hearings** from the menu bar.

The site lists portions of past hearings. At the bottom of each portion, click the **Read more...** link.

Information on the Hearing is listed on a new page. Here you will find the list of witnesses, pertinent documents, testimony and video streaming if available. All of the documents are available in PDF format and you can view the video with any generic video software.

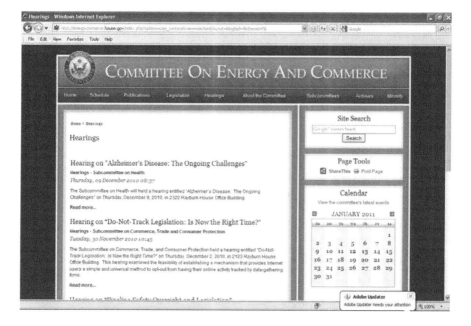

NOTES

NOTES

CONGRESSIONAL STAFF ON CAPITOL HILL

One of the greatest changes on Capitol Hill in the past 40 years has been the growth of congressional staff. In 1960 about 6,000 people worked for the representatives and senators. Congressional reforms in the 1970s increased the work force in Congress to more than 20,000. With the 1994 congressional elections, which resulted in a Republican-controlled Congress in 1995, congressional staff was cut by one-third. Now about 14,000 people work as personal and committee staff, police and maintenance personnel. There is also the staff for the congressional agencies, which are the Congressional Research Service (CRS), Government Accountability Office (GAO) and the Congressional Budget Office (CBO).

Over the years many members of Congress have felt that there are too many staff and too many eager, young people who generate more work. Even though greater staffing expanded the lawmakers' expertise in a broader range of legislative issue areas; in an effort to save money and reduce the size of government the 104th Congress cut the size of the staff. Since the voters asked for less government at the federal level, arguments no longer prevail that the voters and the country as a whole would be better served because of greater staff support.

However, more aides working for a representative or senator, whether personal or committee staff, also means more opportunity for access to a member of Congress. Most contact with the elected officials on Capitol Hill occurs through interaction with their staffs. Members of Congress are too busy to meet with everyone about legislative issues or constituents' problems. Knowing congressional staff on all levels - from caseworkers to chiefs of staff - and developing relationships with them are key to working with the Congress (see chart on following pages).

PROFILE OF CONGRESSIONAL STAFFERS

The reasons why people want to work on Capitol Hill vary as greatly as the 541 members of Congress they serve. Power, influence and self-promotion, even a sense of place in history for some, explain what motivates many people to work very long hours in very cramped offices. However, there has been a recent trend for congressional staff to serve only a short time on Capitol Hill and then to leave to work for lobbyists for almost four times the salary.

The rights and privileges of congressional staff depend on their relationship with the member of Congress for whom they work. Until the 104th Congress workplace laws that applied to the private sector and the federal executive and judiciary branches of government did not apply to Capitol Hill. A staffer could be fired on the spot with no recourse. Although Congress passes laws that affect employer-employee relationships for most Americans, until recently it remained exempt from the legalities of equal employment and affirmative action. It is true that in October 1988, representatives in the House voted overwhelmingly to grant protection under the Civil Rights Act of 1964 to the more than 14,000 persons who work for them. The Office of Fair Employment Practices (OFEP) was established to air employees' complaints. The

Senate eventually followed the House's lead, creating an OFEP in 1992. These offices were meant to function similarly to the Equal Employment Opportunity Commission and other executive branch enforcement agencies, but they were never really that active.

At the beginning of the 104th Congress, lawmakers passed the Congressional Accountability Act that applied nearly a dozen private-sector laws to Congress. Among those included were the Civil Rights Act and Age Discrimination and Rehabilitation Act as well as the Family and Medical Leave Act, the Fair Labor Standards Act and the Occupational Safety and Health Act (OSHA). In 1996, most of the 11 laws went into effect on Capitol Hill.

The low pay and the willingness to work a 60- to 70-hour week with little job protection or promise of promotion suggest that many of the Capitol Hill staff are young. Burnout is so great that the average tenure of service in Congress is less than three years. The accountability of the elected officials for whom they work remains foremost in their minds. Whether personal staff or committee staff these people could lose their jobs if the member who hired them is defeated. Many Democratic House and Senate staffers who served as committee staff for decades found themselves unemployed after the 1994 election when the Republicans won control of the House and the Senate. When the Democrats took control of Congress in 2006, in both the House and the Senate, many Republican committee staff lost their jobs. With the results of the 2010 midterm elections, many House committee staff as well as the personal staffs of more than 60 defeated Democratic House members will lose their jobs because the Democrats are now in the minority.

Always conscious of the scrutiny and power of the voters and interest groups congressional staff are generally courteous and cordial, return phone calls and try to help despite the pressures of their jobs.

Their willingness or reluctance to serve as an extension of the legislator can affect positively or negatively on the public's perception of the elected official.

TYPES OF STAFF ON CAPITOL HILL

There are three categories of staff on the Hill. Generally, personal staff assist a member in the role of representative while the committee staff serve the members in their roles as policy makers. Personal staff work in each of the offices of the 541 representatives and senators. Committee staff, generally older, more educated and professional, provide input and expertise for legislation drafted by more than 200 committees and subcommittees. Finally, those who work at CRS, GAO, and CBO serve as key information staff, usually behind the scenes, for the Congress in all constituent-related and legislative areas.

Staff on Capitol Hill

Member's Personal Staff

- Chief of Staff/Administrative Assistant
- Executive Secretary
- Legislative Assistants
- Caseworkers
- State/District Office Staff

Committee Staff

- Staff Director
- General Counsel
- Professional Committee Staff
- Administrative Staff

Support Agencies

- Congressional Research Service
- Government Accountability Office
- Congressional Budget Office

Personal Staff

The office of each member operates differently. Some congressional observers have described these offices as "541 small businesses." The atmosphere and work schedule depend totally on how the representative or senator chooses to run his or her office. Usually, every office in both the House and Senate has a chief of staff or an administrative assistant (the "AA"), several legislative assistants, caseworkers, an executive secretary and district office staff.

Chief of Staff/Administrative Assistant

The chief of staff, sometimes called the administrative assistant or AA, ranks highest among staff in the Washington office of an elected official. He or she confers with the member in hiring office staff, setting salary levels and delegating workload. Usually, the chief of staff is quite close to the member and knows well the political pulse and profile of the district or state. An appointment with a chief of staff is nearly like meeting with the representative or senator personally.

Legislative Director

Just about every senate and house personal office staff has a legislative director these days. This individual oversees the work of the legislative assistants but also often takes the lead on the committee issues that affect the senator's state or representative's district.

Legislative Assistants

A legislative assistant, or LA, usually focuses on particular policy issues, such as energy or health. The duties include keeping the member abreast of developments in a specific area, serving as a liaison with the committee staff handling that topic (especially if the member sits on that committee), handling constituent mail concerning the issue and meeting with lobbyists and voters as the member's personal representative for the issue of concern.

Caseworkers

Caseworkers resolve problems and answer inquiries from constituents. A knowledge of federal agencies and departments is required for their job, which can be largely that of finding lost Social Security checks and solving problems with veterans' retirement benefits. Successful constituency service can be measured by these individuals' activities, which include assistance in federal grant applications for a district and publicity for the member if the grant is awarded. Increasingly, caseworkers have been placed in the state or district offices where they are able to deal directly and more personally with constituents' problems.

Press Secretary

This congressional staffer serves as the member's chief spokesperson to the media, writes press releases and organizes press conferences. If citizens, interest groups or federal agencies wish to promote their special issue, they direct newsletters, correspondence and reports to this aide.

Executive Secretary/Scheduler

Executive secretaries can be among the most important people in terms of gaining access to an elected official. These personal staff aides make the appointments and juggle the members' unpredictable schedules.

District/State Offices

Every representative to the House has at least one office in his or her district; each senator has several offices to serve his or her state. These offices, often located in a federal building, work directly on the local problems of constituents and increasingly are handling casework for the members. Located in the home area, close to the voters, these offices respond directly to the voters of the district or state.

These are the people to work with if a citizens' group or association wishes to invite its lawmaker to speak or participate in a local conference. A personal tour of a local medical facility, school or factory can help considerably in promoting desired legislation. If the elected official cannot accept an invitation, the director of the district office may attend instead.

House Personal Staff

Each of the 441 members of the House of Representatives is allowed to have a paid staff of no more than 18 full-time and four part-time employees to serve in both the Washington and district offices. The total amount of money each year for the salaries of these staffers and overall office expenses for each representative and senator varies from office to office. Travel allowances for members and their staffs are higher for those who live further from Washington than those who live closer to the nation's capital. Most representatives return some of this money at the end of each year and often do not hire all of the staff to which they are entitled. The average salary of a personal staffer in the House is about $50,000. As of 2009, no personal House staff member may make more than $168,411.

Many of these people are just out of college or graduate school and are aggressive, ambitious and eager to serve the member well. At the same time they promote themselves, often seeming somewhat arrogant. One former Hill staffer, who went to work in the congressional liaison office of a federal department, commented, "I never realized how obnoxious and abrasive we appeared to be until I left the Hill. Now when I call a member's office on behalf of the executive branch agency, I am often shocked by the cockiness of the staffers in the members' offices, many of whom I know are much younger than I." On the whole, however, most of these people try to respond as quickly and as best as they can to requests made by the public and especially by the district.

When a representative is first elected to Congress, all of the staff in Washington may come from the home district. Often these loyal campaign workers, who served the nominee well back home, find life in Washington too expensive or inhospitable and soon return home perhaps to serve in a district office. Of course, members try to have staff who are from the district, especially for the AA position. However, experienced caseworkers whose members were defeated in the November elections can often find jobs in new members' offices because they know the federal agencies well and realize the value of accurate and timely response to constituent needs.

Responding to constituent mail has become more important than ever on Capitol Hill. With the growth of the federal government, and its extension into people's lives, the representatives increasingly play the role of "ombudsman" for their constituents. In the complex American society of the twenty-first century the representative *is* the U.S. government for many of the voters in his or her district. A quick resolution to the problem of a student loan payment or a stolen passport for one voter can mean more votes in the next election as the news spreads among friends and neighbors that "our representative in Washington took care of my problem with the government."

In summary, the personal staff of a member of the House of Representatives exists to work for the reelection of the member whose defeat would mean the loss of their own jobs. As a result, these people work hard to serve and respond to the needs of the district. Following the 2010 midterm elections there were more than 1000 people who worked on the personal staffs for House Democrats who lost their jobs.

Senate Personal Staff

The Senate rules on the number of personal staff differ from those of the House. Since each senator represents an entire state, a Senate office budget for staff hiring depends on the state's population. The senators of

California may each have a personal staff of about 100, while Sen. Tom Carper of Delaware may have only about 40 between his Washington and state offices. In addition to the chief of staff and legislative assistants, there is often a director of legislative affairs in a senator's office whose job is to coordinate the senator's legislative positions and program. Most senators' Washington offices also have a chief counsel, a lawyer, whose job is to offer the senator and staff legal advice and is often a legal expert in subject areas of interest to the senator such as tax or environmental law.

Most senators have several state offices where nearly all of the caseworkers on his or her staff are located. Although responsive to constituent needs, the senator, representing an entire state for six years, does not have the closeness with the voters that a representative has who is up for reelection every two years. The average salary for senate personal staff is $52,000. As of 2009, no Senate personal staff member could earn more than $169,459.

Because of the size of a senator's personal staff aides often do not even know the senator much less have any kind of personal rapport, unlike that which often exists in the House.

COMMITTEE STAFF ON CAPITOL HILL

The people whose primary job is to assist the representatives and senators in their jobs as legislators are the committee staff on Capitol Hill. Even with the reforms in the House of Representatives for the 104th Congress that reduced the number of committees in that chamber, there are still more than 200 committees and subcommittees on Capitol Hill. In further efforts for reform and to save money, both the House and the Senate reduced by one-third the size of their committee staffs in 1995.

On the whole, the committee staff is older, more educated and more professional than the personal staff. They are also better paid. The chairperson of a committee, as in the case of the representative or senator's personal office, decides how much each staff is paid. The size of staff is often determined by the size of a committee's allotted budget from the leadership. In recent years the House Ways and Means and Senate Finance Committees, the tax committees on Capitol Hill, had budgets of more than eight million dollars while the Small Business Committees in Congress had budgets of less than three million.

Many of these people have law degrees or advanced degrees in specialized areas such as tax, economics or engineering. Some staff leave careers in the executive branch such as the Navy, the National Park Service, or the Forest Service. Others may also be academics or former lobbyists who choose to work on Capitol Hill to be closer to the policy-making process. They provide the lawmakers with substantive information and background for proposed legislation. Some of them actually draft the bills and resolutions proposed by lobbying groups, the administration or by the members themselves.

Until the 1994 congressional elections when the Republicans won control of the House for the first time in 40 years, there were Democratic committee staffers in the House and the Senate who had worked on the same committee or subcommittee for nearly 20 years. Such long tenure of service made these committee aides the source of legislative history and background on programs in the face of a changing Congress. Because these committee positions are not permanent, the Republican capture of the Congress in 1994 brought many new staffers to the committees who had not worked on Capitol Hill before.

When the Democrats regained control of the House and the Senate in 2006, many former Democratic committee staff members returned as well. The House Republican return as majority party as a result of the 2010 midterm elections, will mean fewer Democratic committee staff members to serve the minority.

Depending on a committee's rules and budget the chairperson and members of a subcommittee hire and fire the staff who work for him or her. Controversy can arise over a subcommittee's budget for staff hiring, especially when the chairperson of the full committee is powerful and at odds with a subcommittee chairperson. In the 104th Congress there was general agreement on both sides of Capitol Hill that committees' budgets would be lower in order to reduce the size of staff.

Most of the committees have both a majority staff and a separate minority staff. Having greater power because they are the majority, the Republican committee staffers, especially in the House, will play larger roles in setting the legislative agendas. Both in the House and the Senate, they also advise the committee members during the hearings and mark-up sessions, and assist in the floor debate during final consideration of a bill.

Traditionally, there is much more collegiality and cooperation among majority and minority staff in the Senate because of this institution's operations by "unanimous consent." In 2001 when the membership of the Senate was briefly tied at 50 Republicans and 50 Democrats, it was decided that the parties' committee staffs would be equal in number. Even when the Senate was 51 Republicans, 48 Democrats and one Independent in the 108th Congress (2003-2004), the committee staff sizes remained equal between Republicans and Democrats. Because the Republicans picked up seats in the 2004 elections, as the majority party they had larger committee staffs and budgets to hire them. The Democrats' return to power in the Senate following the 2006 midterm elections meant more committee staff for their side of the aisle.

Promotion of legislation and access to the committee members are possible through contact with the committee staff. The staff director and the general counsel could be described as the political staff - those people who are closely allied with the chairperson and work with interest groups, committee staffers on the other side of the Hill and agency officials to facilitate or obstruct the passage of legislation.

The professional staff provide the expertise essential for drafting legislation. As policy specialists in a particular area these aides suggest alternatives to a legislative measure often as a means of compromise with the House or the wishes of the administration.

The administrative staff arrange the hearing rooms, organize the office and publications and oversee the committee's budget and expenses.

Finally, most committees have a press secretary who writes news releases about a committee's agenda to encourage and promote media coverage of hearings both on Capitol Hill and in the congressional districts across the country.

Legislative Support Agencies

Another group of staff serving the members of Congress are those people who work for CRS, GAO and CBO. As additional sources of information for legislation and investigation for the senators and representatives the professional staff of these agencies offer expertise in just about all areas of public policy from MX missiles to taxes to the savings and loan crisis to environmental studies. Unlike the personal and committee staff aides, these professional staff are nonpartisan and are hired to give objective advice and information to any member of Congress who makes a request. These staffs have permanent jobs with GS job classification equivalent to the federal government's civil service.

Congressional Research Service

Established originally in 1914 as the Legislative Reference Service for the Library of Congress, CRS employs about 450 professional staff who respond to thousands of inquiries and requests from the Congress each year. Having the resources of the Library of Congress at their disposal (the best and largest depository of its kind in the world), the CRS

staff provide the elected officials as well as the congressional committees with information needed to draft, review or investigate legislation. As the expertise and reputation of its staff have grown, CRS has been increasingly called on to offer in-depth analysis and review of issues to committees.

Government Accountability Office

Known from its creation in 1921 as the General Accounting Office, it was renamed the Government Accountability Office in 2004. The largest of the support agencies, employing about 3500 people, the GAO was created with the passage of the Budget and Accounting Act. This agency reviews and audits the operations of programs implemented by executive branch agencies established by Congress and is known as the "watchdog" of Congress. During the years of tighter fiscal constraints, its role of investigation and oversight grew. Originally employing only accountants GAO now hires hundreds of other professionals such as scientists, physicians, economists and business management experts. On-site investigations of executive branch activities in Washington, across the country and

GAO

United States Government Accountability Office
Report to the Chairman, Committee on Natural Resources, House of Representatives

May 2008

OFFSHORE MARINE AQUACULTURE

Multiple Administrative and Environmental Issues Need to Be Addressed in Establishing a U.S. Regulatory Framework

GAO

around the world are either self-initiated or at the request of members of Congress.

The comptroller general of the United States directs this agency, reports of which frequently provide Congress with information challenging the activities and operation of the executive branch. Appointed by the President with the advice and consent of the Senate, the comptroller general's term of office is 15 years.

Congressional Budget Office

The newest of the congressional support agencies is the CBO which was established in 1974 with the passage of the Budget and Impoundment Control Act. Employing about 230 people its reputation for excellence in budget and economic matters has grown steadily over the past decade. Working primarily for the budget, tax and appropriations committees of the House and Senate CBO's economists and fiscal specialists analyze economic data, make projections on the national budget deficit and provide the lawmakers with information as they work on the federal budget.

Acting only in an advisory capacity CBO offers Congress the budgetary and economic expertise that the Office of Management and Budget (OMB) provides the President. Increasingly controversial during the Reagan administration CBO has projected deficits and economic downturns contrary to what the directors of OMB have predicted. This office also projected in 1994 that the health care plan proposed by the Clinton administration was not affordable.

The Speaker of the House of Representatives and the President Pro Tempore of the Senate jointly appoint the CBO Director after considering recommendations from the two budget committees. The term of office is four years with no limit on the number of terms a director may serve. Either House of Congress, however, may remove the director by resolution. At the expiration of a term of office the person serving as director may continue in the position until his or her successor is appointed.

Summary

It cannot be denied that the influence and power of staff on Capitol Hill have grown in the past 40 years. Their crucial role as conduits of information to the elected officials is a vital element in making public policy on Capitol Hill. As Congress reduces the size of staff to save money, it also reduces its sources of information. This may mean a greater reliance on federal agency staff, lobbyists and think tanks.

NOTES

THE PRESIDENT AS LEGISLATOR

The President's power to veto legislation passed by the Congress as well as his need to seek the advice and consent of the Senate to ratify treaties with foreign countries have always been felt on Capitol Hill. However, in the twentieth century Presidents began to take a more active role in the legislative process.

U.S. Presidents since 1900, believing that they represent all of the American people, have established themselves more in congressional activities by initiating and orchestrating a legislative agenda for Capitol Hill to act on. New Freedom, New Deal, New Frontier and Reaganomics are names of presidential legislative programs that became the slogans of various administrations. This chapter will examine the evolution of the President as legislator in the following ways: greater familiarity with Capitol Hill, development of a lobbying staff within the White House and the executive agencies and control over the national budget.

THE CHIEF EXECUTIVE AND CAPITOL HILL

George Washington and John Adams complied with Article II, Section 3, of the Constitution by personally giving the State of the Union address before both houses of the Congress. Our third President,

Thomas Jefferson, was a very ineffective public speaker and rather than deliver the speech himself he had it read before Congress. The separation of powers in legislative matters was evident for more than a century.

It was not until Woodrow Wilson, a historian who knew the tradition of the first two Presidents, that the President once again returned to Capitol Hill to review with Congress the state of the union and to outline a legislative program. This physical presence of the chief executive within the halls of Congress meant a greater involvement of the President in the legislative process.

Almost every President since Wilson has gone to Capitol Hill at times other than the delivery of the State of the Union address to promote his legislative programs. In fact, not all of the twentieth century Presidents were unknown within the halls of Congress. Nine of the 20 presidents since 1900 served on Capitol Hill. However, being a former member of the House or Senate has not necessarily ensured that a legislative program passed easily through the Congress. Some Presidents who were total outsiders to Capitol Hill have had the greatest legislative successes.

Consider the cases of Franklin D. Roosevelt and Ronald Reagan, former governors. Neither of these men had ever been elected to Congress, yet each of them had incredible legislative victories on the Hill. During the now famous "first 100 days" of the Roosevelt administration in 1933 Congress passed major pieces of legislation proposed by Roosevelt. In the spring and summer of 1981 Ronald Reagan implemented his Reaganomics program even with a Republican minority in the House of Representatives. Reagan managed to unite the conservative Democrats with the Republicans in the House to defeat the Democrats on the budget and tax bills. Reagan knew how to court elected officials for a vote.

Another former governor, Jimmy Carter, did not fare so well. Having run for the office of President in the wake of Watergate and against the

Washington establishment Carter did not see the importance of seeking the cooperation and the advice of the Democratic leaders on Capitol Hill to carry out his legislative program. Too concerned with the details and the "rightness" of his legislative package rather than with the interests and the personalities of the lawmakers themselves, Carter had an extremely difficult time on the Hill even with a Democratic majority in both the House and the Senate.

Both John F. Kennedy and Lyndon B. Johnson had served in Congress, but Johnson was far more successful in getting the Civil Rights Bill of 1964 and the Great Society programs through Congress. Some analysts say that the congressional opposition to his programs that Kennedy had encountered was beginning to turn around at the time of his assassination.

Like Kennedy Johnson had served in the House and Senate, but Johnson had been majority leader in the Senate. He knew well the strategies of the legislative process and how to use them on certain members of Congress at crucial times. He felt comfortable meeting with the powerful committee chairpersons of both the House and the Senate to seek their advice while at the same time convincing them to vote with him.

Today, with the diffusion of power among the more than 200 committee and subcommittee chairpersons, the personal touches and interviews of a Johnson-style presidency are all that more difficult to achieve. However, major victories are still possible on Capitol Hill. The legislative successes of Ronald Reagan during his first year of office reflect his warm and personable style, a stark contrast to Carter's colder and technical approach. Combining good personal rapport with a well-organized and well-managed Office of Congressional Relations Ronald Reagan achieved significant legislative victories on Capitol Hill.

George H.W. Bush, a former House member, continued the more personal style of Reagan and in a less confrontational way than his predecessor. By inviting members of Congress to informal gatherings in the first family's living quarters Bush tried to maintain a positive, open-door relationship with the legislative branch. Different budget priorities between the Bush White House and the Democrat-controlled Congress contributed to the breakdown of congressional relations that began so well.

Although he was an outsider in Washington, D.C., Bill Clinton met with unusually high legislative successes during the first session of the 103rd Congress largely because of the Democrat-controlled Congress. However, despite the fact that the Democrats controlled both the legislative and executive branches of government, Clinton's controversial health care plan failed to pass during the second session of the 103rd Congress.

The Clinton administration experienced extreme difficulties with the 104th Republican-controlled Congress: The government shut down twice because of disagreements over the budget and spending priorities in 1996 just prior to the elections. Despite these difficulties the President signed into law welfare reform legislation, a minimum wage increase and the Kennedy-Kassebaum health care bill that made health insurance portable when an employee changed jobs.

In the summer of 1997, during the first session of the 105th Congress, the White House and Congress, still controlled by the Republicans, signed an agreement to balance the budget by the year 2002. Indeed, by the time that Bill Clinton left office, the federal budget was more than balanced. It had been in a surplus position for more than three years because of cuts in some government spending and the capital gains taxes sent to the treasury from a booming stock market in the late 1990s.

Although the Republicans retained control over the House during George W. Bush's years as President, the White House's relationship with the U.S. Senate proved to be an unsettled one. Every year the House overwhelmingly approved Bush's legislative agenda of tax cuts, revised energy policy, education reform, tort and bankruptcy reform. Some, but not all, of these issues succeeded in Bush's first term. For the President's tax cuts, his "No Child Behind Left Behind" education initiative, the post 9/11 national security legislation and the Healthy Forest Restoration Act the Senate agreed enough with the House to pass these bills. Even though there was agreement between both houses of Congress on tort and bankruptcy reform early in Bush's second term, the Republican-controlled Senate of 2005-2006 remained at odds with the White House and the House over cuts in Medicaid and food stamp programs, long-term energy policy, and national security issues.

During the final two years of the George W. Bush presidency (2007-2008), stalemate pretty much controlled the legislative process because the Democrats won back control of both the House and the Senate in 2006. President Bush began to veto bills, sometimes several times, as in the case of the state run health care bill for children known as SCHIP.

The American people elected Barack Obama, a Democrat, to the White House in 2008. His party also increased its majorities in the House and Senate that year as well. As a matter of fact, Democrats held 60 seats in the Senate for about six months in 2009 which meant a filibuster-proof chamber. But this President and his party also inherited the worst economic crisis in the country since the 1930s.

With these large majorities on Capitol Hill President Obama signed in to law major pieces of legislation ranging from the stimulus for economic recovery to health care reform to financial institution reforms to consumer credit card protection with little or no support from the Republicans on Capitol Hill. However, despite all of these important legislative victories, unemployment remained at nearly 10% in November of 2010 when the Democrats lost more than 60 seats in the House of Representatives at the midterm elections that year.

THE WHITE HOUSE LOBBIES ON CAPITOL HILL

As each twentieth century President's involvement in the legislative process grew, it naturally followed that an executive branch lobbying staff would develop. During the Eisenhower administration the Office of Congressional Relations was formally set up in the White House.

In addition to a team of lobbyists whose job over the years has been purely political, Presidents have turned to the legislative affairs staffs in the executive departments and agencies to develop the policy for their legislative programs and to assist in legislative liaison on the Hill.

Congress, often ambivalent about lobbying by the executive branch departments and agencies, has realized over the years that information freely exchanged is vital for the legislative process in a democracy. In fact, the Hill frequently seeks the advice and programmatic expertise of career civil servants.

DWIGHT EISENHOWER TO GERALD FORD

It was not until the Eisenhower administration that an office of congressional relations was established in a formal way at the White

House. The President wanted such an office not for the purpose of promoting his legislative program on Capitol Hill, but rather to keep the Republican members of Congress, who controlled both the House and the Senate in 1952, from asking for political favors from the President.

Lawrence O'Brien, whom John F. Kennedy selected to head the Office of Congressional Relations in 1960, established this office as a lobbying arm for the chief executive. Having worked with Kennedy since 1952 O'Brien knew well the give and take of the political scene. He set the precedent for successful White House liaison with Capitol Hill: Political rather than substantive expertise was required of a staff who would build coalitions among the various factions of Congress.

Even though the Democrats controlled both the House and the Senate in 1960, passage of the liberal New Frontier program was not easy. O'Brien recognized and dealt with the political realities of conservative southern Democrats in the House and a minority of northern Democrats in the Senate. Such a philosophical makeup made O'Brien and his team of lobbyists organize along geographical lines rather than on issues.

In addition to organizing a lobbying team that worked directly for the White House O'Brien also set the precedent for success with Congress by working closely with the executive departments' legislative staffs, the Democratic leadership on the Hill and the interest groups that favored the President's program. He remained the director of this office under President Lyndon Johnson after Kennedy's death. The

John Ehrlichman

Counsel and Assistant to the President for Domestic Affairs under President Richard Nixon. A key figure in the Watergate scandal for which he was convicted of conspiracy, obstruction of justice and perjury. He served a year and a half in prison for his crimes.

H.R. Haldeman

White House Chief of Staff to President Richard Nixon. Found guilty of conspiracy and obstruction of justice for his role in Watergate. He was imprisoned for 18 months for his crimes.

combination of his organizational skills with that of LBJ's own political prowess meant the passage of stalled civil rights legislation and the Great Society program.

Richard Nixon and Gerald Ford both knew highs and lows in dealing with the Hill. Nixon frequently expressed his displeasure with Congress and its inability to accomplish its legislative business. Although he had served in the House, the Senate and as vice president, Nixon did not like the political bargaining that is so vital in working with Capitol Hill. He sometimes bypassed the legislative process by using executive privilege as in impounding funds for programs appropriated by Congress.

Bryce Harlow, Clark MacGregor and William Timmons served as directors of Nixon's Office of Congressional Relations. Conflict between their office and that of Nixon's chief advisers, John Ehrlichman and H. R. Haldeman, did not help promote a legislative program on Capitol Hill. By the beginning of his second term, with Haldeman and Ehrlichman having resigned, Nixon did begin to meet with the Republican congressional leaders on a more regular basis in an effort to cooperate more fully with the Hill.

Gerald Ford's legislative team faced the difficult days following Watergate as well as a Democrat-controlled Congress. Ford chose Max Friedersdorf to lead the Office of Congressional Relations, which played more of a policy-making role during Ford's short administration. Lacking a majority in either house of Congress Ford's legislative successes on the Hill were exhibited more in blocking veto overrides than implementing legislation.

JIMMY CARTER TO GEORGE W. BUSH

The White House lobbying effort on the Hill continued along geographical lines throughout the Johnson, Nixon and Ford

Information Resources in the Administration and Congress

President	Congress

1,300,000 Professional People on Federal Payroll

14,000 Professional People on Legislative Payroll

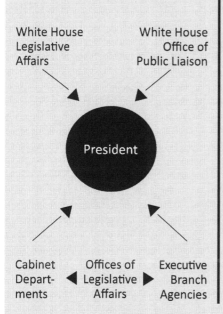

White House Legislative Affairs

White House Office of Public Liaison

President

Cabinet Departments ◄ Offices of Legislative Affairs ► Executive Branch Agencies

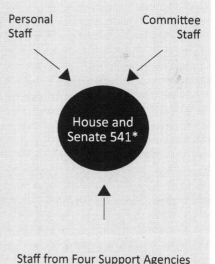

Personal Staff

Committee Staff

House and Senate 541*

Staff from Four Support Agencies

*There are six nonvoting delegates in the House from Guam, the Virgin Islands, American Samoa, Puerto Rico, the Northern Mariana Islands and the District of Columbia.

administrations. Cultivating relationships with certain leading representatives and senators meant a better knowledge of these politicians as people who, as elected officials, had certain district and state needs that had to be kept in mind.

Since Jimmy Carter had run against the Washington establishment in 1976, he did not feel that he owed any allegiance to anyone. Issues of public policy, and not the policymakers themselves, were more important. As a result Carter organized his Office of Congressional Relations along issue lines. The director of this office was Frank Moore who, like Carter, was an outsider to Washington and its ways of doing business.

Believing that he could convince the members of Congress to vote purely on the merits of a piece of legislation without any consideration of projects for a representative's or senator's district or state, Carter never established a good rapport with Congress. Although he had later legislative successes, such as the ratification of the Panama Canal treaties, the "windfall" profits tax on oil companies and the deregulation of some transportation companies, the perception that Carter's legislative team could not competently deal with Congress remained until the end of his administration.

Ronald Reagan learned from Jimmy Carter's mistakes. Although he had never participated in the Washington scene, Reagan chose Max Friedersdorf, who had worked for Gerald Ford, to head his Office of Congressional Relations. Through the incredible efforts of Friedersdorf and his team of geographically organized lobbyists President Reagan's legislative program for tax and budget reform was implemented in the summer of 1981. All lobbyists had either congressional or lobbying experience. Although achieving more legislative victories in Reagan's first term than in the second President Reagan's Office of Congressional Relations had a better relationship and knew greater successes on Capitol

Hill than his predecessor's.

George H. W. Bush's Office of Congressional Relations (1989-1992), which was composed of eight professional staff, worked both sides of Capitol Hill. Much legislation opposed by the President was passed by the Democrat-controlled Congress. As political consensus and comity broke down during the Bush presidency, George H.W. Bush successfully vetoed 46 bills.

With the election of Bill Clinton, a Democrat, in 1992 as well as Democratic control of both the House and the Senate during the 103rd Congress for the ensuing two years, the White House achieved many legislative successes on Capitol Hill. These ranged from deficit reduction to the passage of the North American Free Trade Agreement to the Family Leave Bill. When the Republicans took control of Congress in 1994, relations between the White House and Capitol Hill broke down. Fights over the budget resulted in two federal government shutdowns. Investigations of President's Clinton's investment in an Arkansas land deal, his funding for his re-election bid in 1996 and finally his impeachment by the House in 1998 over the Monica Lewinsky affair stalled much of his legislative agenda on Capitol Hill during his second term. However, Clinton successfully vetoed 36 bills passed by Congress during his presidency, only two of which were overridden by Congress.

With the controversial election of George W. Bush to the White House in 2000 along with a largely Republican Congress there was much optimism that much could be done legislatively for the conservative agenda. Indeed, many tax cuts passed both houses of Congress along with the post 9/11 national security legislation that included the Benefits to Public Safety Officers Act, the Authorization for Use of Military Force, the Airline Transportation and Systems Stabilization Act and the Patriot Act. Initially, the Bush administration was quite open in dealing with the

Members of Congress. It invited members of both parties to the White House for meetings. President Bush gave nicknames to a favored few. But in the wake of the war in Iraq disagreements over budget and tax cuts, the suspected breaches in national security by the White House in the Valery Plame affair, the George W. Bush White House became increasingly closed to dialog with Capitol Hill and the press. This President Bush's office of legislative affairs had a staff of 24 people. President Bush vetoed a total of ten bills in eight years, three of which were successfully overridden by the Democratically controlled 110th Congress.

PRESIDENT OBAMA

On Inauguration Day, January 20, 2009, Barak Obama became the 44th president of the United States. He is the first African-American elected to this office in the country's history. He also assumed power with larger majorities in the House and Senate. In an effort to work better with Capitol Hill his White House hired a number of former congressional staff people whose previous bosses would be influential members of the 111th Congress. Chosen to run the White House Office of Legislative Affairs was Phil Schrilo, the former chief of staff for Henry Waxman, the new chairman of the powerful House Energy and Commerce Committee. This committee took the lead on the issues of climate change and health care reform legislation both of which passed the House of Representatives. With a great amount of political capital expended, the health care reform bill was signed in to law; the climate change issue died in the Senate.

As a result of the 2010 midterm elections when the Republicans took control of the House, the Obama White House made several staff changes when Jacob Lew became Chief of Staff and Rob Nabors became the Director of the White House Office of Legislative Affairs.

EXECUTIVE BRANCH LIAISON WITH LEGISLATIVE BRANCH

The offices of legislative affairs in the departments and agencies throughout the executive branch work with the White House domestic policy staff, a group of counselors which develops a legislative agenda strictly for national issues. These agencies work for the chief executive whose legislative agenda they must support. These legislative offices are legally forbidden to participate in or promote a grass-roots lobby of voters to pressure members of Congress on a piece of legislation. In a society where the free exchange of information is related to the open and democratic process, the line between public relations or department liaison and outright lobbying can be a fine one. Many departments, such as the Navy, the Army and the Office of Personnel Management, have offices of legislative affairs in the House and Senate office buildings. Thus, their staffs can educate representatives, senators and their

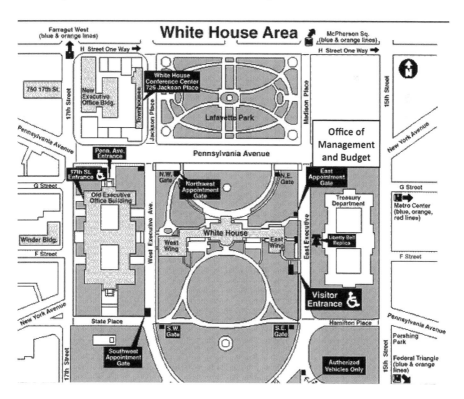

staffs about various programs.

The executive departments' legislative affairs staffs also work closely with the White House Office of Congressional Relations and domestic policy counsels to coordinate legislation and to encourage a single, united effort and voice for the administration. Frequently headed by political appointees (Schedule Cs) who have Hill contacts, these legislative affairs offices draw on the knowledge and expertise of thousands of career civil servants in designing policy for the President's legislative program.

The strong inducement of the executive branch in crafting the makeup of legislative affairs staffs has been vital to a strong voice on the Hill. Jimmy Carter chose to let the department's secretary appoint his or her own legislative staffs. As a result, some people in his administration felt that an agency's liaison staff worked more for their department's programs than for the administration as a whole. Since the years of Ronald Reagan the Office of Management and Budget (the President's budget office) has emerged as the major coordinator for the President's legislative agenda.

THE PRESIDENT AND THE NATIONAL BUDGET

President Ronald Reagan won legislative victories in the areas of budget and tax not only because of his popularity and successful lobbying, but also because the evolution and influence of the office of the President in this century has meant a greater role for the President as manager of the entire government. As the leading "executive" officer he should have input into the makeup of the national budget.

Article I, Section 7 of the Constitution clearly states that revenue-raising legislation begins in the House of Representatives (*All bills for raising Revenue shall originate in the House of Representatives;*). However, congressional response to an executive branch legislative agenda involving the areas of budget and tax has become the way of lawmaking in this century.

When the House established the Committee on Ways and Means as a permanent committee in 1794, it provided itself with an institutional means to oversee the national purse. Over the next 100 years (with the exception of the Civil War) the Congress remained the dominant branch of government and controlled the business of the state through tariffs and tax measures. With the development in the 1820s of today's system of standing committees on the Hill the President's influence in the legislative process weakened. Power in the Congress was diffused among the committee chairpersons, each of whom had his own legislative agenda.

Such diffusion of power through the committee system, while strengthening the Congress in the nineteenth century, has weakened it today because the executive branch has an authority and stature that it did not have 100 years ago.

Between 1870 and 1920, the United States was involved in, and won, two wars, the Spanish-American War and World War I. As commander-in-chief during these crises the President's stature increased along with governmental services and expenditures. The number of executive departments and agencies increased, and it was gradually felt by the lawmakers on Capitol Hill that the President as chief executive should oversee the operations and budgets of these bureaus

to have a more responsible government.

In 1921 Congress passed the Budget and Accounting Act, whose purpose was to control agency spending. Each department would be required to submit a projected budget to the Bureau of the Budget (BOB) at the Department of the Treasury. The BOB would make changes and the President would then submit these budgets to Congress for approval. As originally conceived the 1921 act was not perceived by Congress to lessen its power over the national budget.

However, Franklin D. Roosevelt saw government's role differently when his New Deal legislation created even more agencies and regulations for the country. Believing that larger government should indeed be a permanent part of America's future, Roosevelt moved the BOB from the Department of the Treasury to the executive office of the President. By establishing direct White House control over the government's budget the President would then propose a legislative program on Capitol Hill for Congress to fund executive branch activities. Thus began the Congress's role of responding to rather than initiating budget requests.

SUMMARY

The President of the United States is involved more than ever before in the legislative process on Capitol Hill. His term of four years is twice as long as that of any one member of the House of Representatives. All of whose members are up for reelection every two years. The growth in the size, strength and stability of the executive office of the President since 1900 has enabled it to bridge the gap between the executive and legislative branches of government. Such efficiency by the executive branch has not, however, evolved into an executive tyranny, because in this country the nation's leader still must answer to the inefficient but watchful other end of Pennsylvania Avenue, Capitol Hill.

NOTES

NOTES

THE FEDERAL BUDGET AND THE CONGRESSIONAL BUDGET PROCESS

In 1974 Congress passed the Budget and Impoundment Control Act in an effort to influence the course and content of the national budget. Reacting to the power of the "imperial presidencies" of Lyndon B. Johnson and Richard Nixon as well as negative public opinion toward Washington in the wake of the Vietnam conflict and Watergate, the lawmakers on Capitol Hill felt that the legislative branch needed to reassert its constitutional right to control the country's purse strings. Responding to presidential initiatives, especially in budget matters, and not proposing its own throughout the 1960s had eroded the power of Congress over the budget. In the years prior to 1974, power was only in a few places on Capitol Hill and this enabled the White House to deal with only a few members, particularly senior members of Congress, to pass its programs.

During the years when the economics of deficit spending was the national way of government business, both for Republican and Democratic presidents, there were no committees on the Hill monitoring the bottom line of expenditures versus revenues. Programs were created by the authorizing committees, funded by the appropriations committees and implemented by the executive branch with little regard for tax revenues to pay for the government's services. Along with this near automatic budget approval process on Capitol Hill both the Johnson and Nixon administrations oversaw the creation of new entitlement programs which meant greater government spending for people's needs. Johnson's Great Society initiatives such as Medicare and Medicaid, and President Nixon's entitlement programs of General Revenue Sharing, the Comprehensive Employment and Training Act and Community Development exemplify the chief executive's legislative successes on Capitol Hill in those years. These victories meant greater government spending. It was not until the passage of the Budget Act in 1974 that Congress established "tally sheets" to consider the budget.

The lack of institutional means to oversee the budget combined with the impoundment of funds by Nixon led concerned lawmakers to conceive and pass the Budget Act of 1974. The act made these changes:

- The fiscal year (FY) would begin on October 1 rather than July 1 to give Congress more time to study and discuss the budget.
- House and Senate budget committees would be established to set economic priorities by making spending recommendations to the appropriations and revenue-raising (tax) committees and thereby impose a discipline on the budgeting process.
- The Congressional Budget Office (CBO) would be created to provide Congress with data and objective in-house advice for spending and taxes. (CBO serves Congress in much the same manner as the Office of Management and Budget [OMB] serves the President.)
- Congress would have the right to review and approve proposed presidential impoundment of funds.
- Congress would follow a timetable for budget passage.

Over 35 years have passed since Congress began working within the guidelines of the budget process. What this process is, how it has changed in the past three decades and how it works will be outlined on the following pages.

THE FEDERAL BUDGET AND THE EXECUTIVE BRANCH

The formulation of the President's budget begins about 19 months before the fiscal year under consideration. This means that in March 2011 the executive branch begins planning for the 2013 budget, which takes effect on October 1, 2012.

Each year in the late winter and early spring bureaucrats in the executive branch's agencies and departments submit their requests to their program and budget offices for activities they wish to be funded. After many months of negotiations among the White House, OMB and the agencies, the President's budget is submitted to Capitol Hill in early February of each year.

What Congressional and Executive Agency Processes Are Going on in FY 2013

| October - December
Start of New Fiscal Year	January - February	March - June	July - September
	Congressional Review of agencies FY 2012 accomplishments.		
Fiscal Year 2013 Begins.	Executives agencies implement programs for FY 2013.		
OMB Reviews agency requests for FY 2014 and issues pasbacks; agency appeals to OMB and/or President. Final decisions.	Compiliation and printing of executive budget request for FY 2014. President submits budget request to Congress no later than the first Monday in February.	Congressional consideration of the President's budget request begins. March 15 Committees submit views and estimates on the budget to budget committee. April 15 Deadline for adopting the budget resolution for FY 2014.	Appropriations process (Congress writes budget). May - July House action on regular appropriations bills for FY 2014. July - September Senate action and conference on regular appropriations; enactment of appropriations.
Field offices developing budget estimates for FY 2015.		Development of budget guidelines and preliminary policies. Call for estimates issued by agency budget office to operating units.	Agencies formulate detailed request for FY 2015, which are submitted to OMB.

If the United States had a parliamentary form of government, approval of the budget by the legislative branch would be immediate. The chief executive in parliamentary government holds his position because he is the leader of the party that has the majority of seats in the lawmaking body of the government. Under this system, however, there is no separation of powers between the executive and legislative branches like that which exists in the United States.

The Constitution calls for the legislative branch to be the revenue-raising arm of the government. Over the years Congress has become very involved in the appropriating process. Thus, a federal budget that is submitted to Capitol Hill with the politics and legislative agenda of one individual behind it, the President, encounters the legislative agendas and parochial interests of the 541 members of Congress.

CONGRESSIONAL BUDGET PROCESS

The guidelines established by the 1974 Budget Act called for a series of steps that, at the time, included procedures that would set total budget targets for the next fiscal year. The process laid out a series of date-specific deadlines, starting in March and ending in September, for the lawmakers to meet over a six-month period considering the budget.

For the first few fiscal years following 1974 Congress kept to its timetable. The members in both houses of Congress took the schedule quite seriously. Even Sen. John Stennis, who in the mid-1970s was chairperson of both the Senate Armed Services Committee and the Defense Subcommittee on Appropriations, was made to comply with the dates and spending ceilings set by the Senate Budget Committee.

The process did not work well, or smoothly, in the face of growing deficits in the 1980s. Congress, which established this timetable, could ignore it, and this was exactly what happened. With no budget in place by October 1 the government was often funded by continuing resolution. This last-minute scramble and disagreement between Congress and the President over budget priorities led to government shutdowns in the early 1980s, and greatly frustrated executive branch planners whose projects could not be implemented because Congress had not voted the money for the programs.

In an effort to gain better control over the mounting deficit in the 1980s, Congress passed several versions of what became known as the Gramm-Rudman-Hollings Act. With the goal of cutting the deficit to $0 by capping spending on the discretionary, appropriated dollars, not the entitlement programs, Congress hoped to achieve a balanced budget by 1993. Even with this mechanism in place the deficits did not decline.

During George H.W. Bush's presidency deficits continued to mount. Conflicts between Capitol Hill and the White House in finding agreement on a budget solution mounted. In an effort to work for more meaningful control over national spending congressional and presidential budget negotiators finally developed a new process as part of the budget for FY 1991. The 1990 budget agreement called for Congress to pass the Budget Enforcement Act of 1990, which altered the budget process once again.

During fiscal years 1991 to 1993 the government's discretionary spending (yearly appropriated dollars) was divided among defense, domestic and international aid programs. Each category was subject to sequestration (automatic cuts) if the money appropriated over the next three fiscal years exceeded targets set by the budget agreement reached in the fall of 1990. If a congressional committee wanted to increase spending for any program in these three discretionary areas, cuts had to come from other programs in the category, or revenues had to be raised to fund the new spending through taxes or user fees, a "pay as you go" plan.

In fiscal years 1994 and 1995, the three discretionary spending areas were once again faced with automatic cuts if the targets for yearly spending were exceeded. This was the original design of Gramm-Rudman-Hollings in 1985.

Once again, exempt from the automatic budget chopping block were the entitlement programs, such as Social Security and Medicare, the fastest growing budget items. However, the "pay as you go" plan also applied to them and was extended to 2002 in the balanced budget agreement of 1997. If, for example, a committee wished to increase Medicare benefits, fees or taxes must be passed to pay for the new benefits. Operation Desert Storm, the first war with Iraq in 1991, was funded from an account separate from that of defense.

Projection of the programmatic cost estimates as well as the new revenue estimates rests with OMB, the President's budget office. This task belonged to CBO and the Joint Committee on Taxation, information agents of Congress, before the 1990 budget agreement.

It should be noted here that many economists and budget experts argue today that the posture of the federal budget from that of huge deficit to near surplus in 1998 began with these important spending decisions made by Congress and the George H.W. Bush administration in 1990. Faulted by his critics for signing legislation that increased taxes, Bush's responsible decision set the stage for the Clinton administration to continue the downward trend in federal spending. It should also be noted that spending for the annual discretionary appropriated dollars was capped until 2002. Since

the expiration of the caps congressional spending grew for discretionary programs.

When Bill Clinton was elected president, he promised to halve the budget deficit in his first term. The Omnibus Budget Reconciliation Act of 1993 narrowly passed the 103rd Congress. Containing both spending cuts and tax increases this plan for deficit reduction continued to freeze the caps for discretionary appropriated spending for five years or until 1998. The plan did not call for freezes on any of the entitlement programs. No Republican on Capitol Hill voted for this bill.

These actions in 1990 and 1993 by Capitol Hill and the White House along with a robust economy with low unemployment allowed the budget deficit to decline from a record $290 billion in 1992, the last year of George H.W. Bush's presidency, to $0 and to a surplus of $60 billion for FY 1998.

As a result of the congressional elections of 1994 the Republican Party gained control of both the House and Senate for the first time in 40 years. Feeling that the American people wanted less government, the Republicans in the House - guided by their election manifesto, the "Contract with America," that promised a balanced budget by the year 2002 - were determined to cut federal taxes and programs. Republicans in the Senate, not one of whose incumbents signed "the Contract with America," wanted to cut spending before taxes.

In the summer of 1995 Congress managed to cut $25 billion from the budget passed for FY 1995 by voting for a rescission which took back dollars that the 103rd Congress had appropriated for federal agencies for FY 1995. This action proved to be only the start to a major confrontation by the Republican-controlled Congress with the Clinton White House over spending priorities. Disagreements over the budget led not to one but to two government shutdowns in November of 1995 for four days and in December-January of 1995-1996 for three weeks. The White House managed to win the public relations battle with the public who generally blamed this budget impasse on the Republicans in Congress. Election year politics of 1996 pushed both Congress and the President to agree on a budget for FY 1997 by October 1, 1996.

Also in 1996, Congress passed and President Clinton signed into law "The Line-Item Veto Act." It went into effect on January 1, 1997. To the surprise of the Republican leaders in Congress the President used the line-item veto on 81 items, 38 of which Congress overrode. The vetoes on the remaining 43 items were invalidated when the Supreme Court declared the line-item veto unconstitutional in 1998.

Bill Clinton's re-election in 1996, the first Democrat since Lyndon Johnson to be re-elected to the White House, also brought fewer Republicans back to the House. Still led by Newt Gingrich and somewhat chastened by the bad press over the budget battles of 1995 and 1996, Congress and the President managed to work out a budget agreement in the summer of 1997 to balance the budget within five years. Somewhat ahead of schedule due to a thriving economy and low unemployment, which meant an increase in tax revenues as well as some federal spending reduction, the deficit for FY 1998 was $0 with a surplus of $60 billion.

When President Clinton left office in 2001, the federal budget had a surplus of $236 billion with projections of trillions of dollars in surpluses over the next decade. The Clinton Budget plan seemed to have anticipated the retirement needs of the baby-boomer generation to begin in 2011.

George W. Bush entered the White House in 2001 as the nation's 43rd president. The CBO projected a federal budget surplus of over $10 trillion thru 2010. Five years later, this surplus had vanished and annual deficits returned to $300 to $400 billion a year. How did this happen?

Running for president as a fiscal conservative, one of the major planks

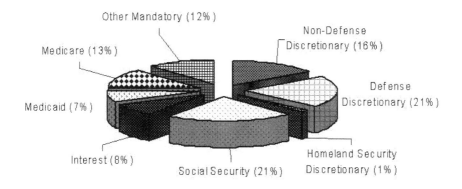

of George W. Bush's campaign platform in 2000 was to cut taxes. Big government runs on large tax revenues. Fiscal conservatives want smaller government which means fewer dollars from the taxpayers. In the spring of 2001, the early months of George W. Bush's presidency, he proposed and Congress passed, with the encouragement of the Federal Reserve Chairman, Alan Greenspan, major tax cuts. Many Americans paid fewer taxes but the highest tax cuts went to the top 1% or the wealthiest people.

What followed, of course, were the September 11 attacks by Al Quaeda in 2001, which opened the U.S. War on Terrorism. Then there were the wars and sustained U.S. military presence in Afghanistan and Iraq starting in 2002 in addition to the recession that began in March of 2001. Also, domestically there was the catastrophic hurricane seasons of 2004 and 2005 which required additional billions of federal dollars in aid that Congress appropriated.

Earmarks

Funds provided by the Congress for projects, programs, or grants where the purported congressional direction (whether in statutory text, report language, or other communication) circumvents otherwise applicable merit-based or competitive allocation processes, or specifies the location or recipient, or otherwise curtails the ability of the executive branch to manage its statutory and constitutional responsibilities pertaining to the funds allocation process.

It should also be recalled that in the context of these international and domestic crises, spending for federal health care (Medicare and Medicaid) and retirement (Social Security, Civil Service, Veterans) programs continued unabated. On top of all of this, however, the Republican-controlled Congress continued to appropriate dollars for domestic programs and special projects (earmarks) for their states and districts. The highway bill signed by President Bush in 2005 contained more than 6000 earmarks.

So to answer the questions of disappearing surpluses there were a combination of domestic and international crises and responsibilities, continued increases in entitlement and discretionary spending with fewer

Civilian Conservation Corps (CCC)

A public work relief program for unemployed men age 18-25, providing unskilled manual labor related to the conservation and development of natural resources in rural areas of the United States from 1933 to 1942. As part of the New Deal legislation proposed by President Franklin D. Roosevelt (FDR), the CCC was designed to provide relief for unemployed youth who had a very hard time finding jobs during the Great Depression while implementing a general natural resource conservation program on public lands in every U.S. state, including the territories of Alaska, Hawaii, Puerto Rico, and the U.S. Virgin Islands.

The CCC became the most popular New Deal program among the general public, providing jobs for a total of 3 million young men from families on relief. Implicitly the CCC also led to awareness and appreciation of the outdoors and the nation's natural resources, especially for city youth. The CCC was never considered a permanent program and depended on emergency and temporary legislation for its existence. On June 30, 1942 Congress voted to eliminate funding for the CCC, formally ceasing active operation of the program.

During the time of the CCC, volunteers planted nearly 3 billion trees to help reforest America, constructed more than 800 parks nationwide that would become the start of most state parks, developed forest fire fighting methods, a network of thousands of miles of public roadways, and constructed buildings connecting the nation's public lands.

taxes to pay for it all.

As has been mentioned in previous chapters, President Barack Obama came to power in 2009 during the worst economic crisis the country had known since the 1930s. To respond to the financial meltdown that occurred in the fall of 2008, President Bush had signed in to law the Troubled Asset Relief Program (TARP) to bailout the failing banks on Wall Street which amounted to nearly $800 billion dollars. To stimulate the economy since unemployment continued to rise, most Democrats in the House and the Senate (Only three Republican senators voted for the bill that had no Republican support in the House) passed the Recovery Act that cost over $800 billion. President Obama signed the bill in to law in February 2009. The purpose of this legislation was to create jobs, to put people to work. These two pieces of legislation added over $1.5 trillion to the debt but was perceived by the American people as only helping the wealthy on Wall Street and failing to ease the unemployment rate that had grown to nearly 10% in the spring of 2009.

As the Republicans take control of the House of Representatives in 2011, believing that they have a mandate to cut government size and spending, the promise of budget fights between the White House and Capitol Hill looms large.

THE FOUR PHASES OF THE BUDGET PROCESS

With the passage of the Budget Enforcement Act in 1990 the 1974 budget process was amended and its timetable was changed. A timetable can be found at the end of this chapter.

1. Executive Budget Goes to Capitol Hill

Congress reconvenes each January. The President submits his budget request for congressional consideration in early February.

With over a year of preparation by the executive branch, the legislative branch now has nearly eight months to examine and pass the budget. All House and Senate standing committees must submit "views and estimates" of expenditures for the coming year to the budget committees within six weeks after the President's submission, the first major deadline in the budget process and also the end of phase one.

Any new program that a department, agency or lobbying or international group may want funded should be in the President's budget when it is sent to the Hill. Executive agencies along with interest groups have ten months to try to incorporate funds for their projects into the budget before the President submits his request to Congress. Funding for new projects after the budget has reached the Hill is very difficult to incorporate. Most programs contained in the executive budget and in the committees' February reports to the budget committees will stay in the proposed budget document.

2. The Budget Resolution

Between late February and April 15, the deadline for passing the budget resolution, the House and Senate budget committees draft their versions of the budget resolution. Desirous of a budget that meets agreed-to targets in both discretionary and entitlement areas, these committees review the standing committees' proposed expenditures, the estimated tax revenues and the CBO budget analysis. Both houses should pass budget resolutions by April 15 with differences between the two resolved in conference committee. If a budget resolution is not reported by this date, the budget committees set spending limits for appropriations committees in discretionary categories that equal those set in the President's original budget submission.

3. The Reconciliation Process

The annual budget resolution may contain directions, called reconciliation instructions, that direct certain committees to report legislation that will reduce entitlements or increase revenues or user fees. They are designed to ensure compliance with the entitlement targets set in the 1993 budget agreement. This process is also a mechanism to try to cut authorized programs or grant new authority such as to drill in the arctic National Wildlife Refuge. In 2005 the Republican-controlled Congress cut nearly $40 billion from entitlement programs such as Medicaid and student loans.

4. Authorization and Appropriation Processes

Most of the work of the House and Senate authorization and appropriations committees takes place between mid-April and mid-September. These committees are also involved in structuring the budget resolution having submitted their views and estimates to the budget committees earlier in the year.

Conflict between the authorizing and appropriating committees may also arise. To be funded a program must be authorized, but this action does not guarantee funding. The appropriations committees may refuse or be unable to fund a program authorized by Congress in order to preserve targets set in a discretionary area for the upcoming fiscal year.

During the spring agency officials appear before the House and Senate appropriations subcommittees to defend their budget requests and to offer plans for the department's future goals. Usually, the full Committee on Appropriations accepts the recommendations of its subcommittees.

By May 15 the House Appropriations Committee may report the annual appropriations bills. The 1990 amendments to the 1974 budget timetable call for Congress to pass all appropriations bills by June 30 leaving the remainder of the summer for conference committees to resolve differences. Rarely have all of these differences over budget matters been resolved by the start on the fiscal year on October 1, the new fiscal year.

It should be noted here that earmarking money for a member of Congress' special projects occurs during the appropriations process. In 2005 there were more than 14,000 earmarks inserted into appropriations bills. This number grew to over 16,000 a year later.

When the Democrats took control of Capitol Hill in January of 2007, they worked to cut the earmarks by half. They also required that there be greater "transparency" in the earmarking process with representatives and senators actually identifying themselves with the specific project requested. It should be pointed out that of the nearly $4 trillion federal budget, earmarks represent less than 5% of the total budget.

THE REALITIES OF THE BUDGET PROCESS ON CAPITOL HILL

Unable to complete its budget work in a timely fashion Congress funded the government on continuing resolutions for most of the 1980s. One notable exception occurred in the wake of the 1987 stock market crash when the 100th Congress passed a budget for FY 1989 before the new fiscal year began.

Not much deficit reduction occurred during the George H.W. Bush Administration. The passage of the Omnibus Budget Reconciliation Act in August 1993, at the beginning of Bill Clinton's presidency, reduced the deficit to around $250 billion from its high of $290 billion in 1992. The caps on the discretionary dollars between 1994 and 1998, set in law by the Omnibus Budget Reconciliation Act of 1993, were honored by both branches of government. This budget discipline, along with the huge taxes into the federal treasury because of the strong U.S. economy in the late

1990s, led to discussion of surpluses and what to do with them.

As was outlined above, the surplus posture of the federal government when the 21st century began and during George W. Bush's presidency from 2001-2008, disappeared.

The reality of the costs of entitlements due the baby-boomer generation has arrived. Many of them have begun to take Social Security at 62 in an era where there is nearly 10% unemployment which also means fewer payroll taxes paid into the Social Security trust fund. As the 112th Congress begins in 2011, controversy between the Republicans on Capitol Hill and Obama's Democratic White House over the size and specifics of the budget is a given. Argument over the size and composition of the federal government in an era of fewer tax dollars with growing fiscal responsibilities by the government to the people will continue.

SUMMARY

The continuing struggle over the budget reflects a lack of national consensus on the federal government's spending priorities. Conflicts arise due to the check-and-balance nature of the government especially concerning who wields power over the national purse - Capitol Hill or the White House.

With the Republicans in control of Capitol Hill for the 104th Congress the legislative branch more aggressively exercised its power of the purse. They believed that they had a mandate in 1995 to cut the size of the federal government by eliminating such federal departments as Energy, Education and Commerce in addition to giving their constituents, the American people, huge tax cuts. All three of these departments still exist today.

The budget talk of surpluses and what to do with them lasted from 1999 to 2001. Now that the posture of the federal budget has returned to deficit status, disagreement on solving the problem of the federal government's spending obligations with fewer tax resources has returned to Washington, DC. Consensus and compromise are at the heart of the democratic form of government; they will be needed by the politicians at both ends of Pennsylvania Avenue over the coming years.

Time Frame	Action
January	Congress convenes
Five days before the President's budget submission	Congressional Budget Office (CBO) submits sequestration preview report
Early February	Congress receives President's budget submission; Office of Management and Budget (OMB) submits sequestration preview report
Within six weeks after President's budget submission	Committees submit views and estimates to House Budget Committee
April 15	Congress completes action on fiscal year budget resolution
April 30	CBO and Treasury Department report on financial soundness of government-sponsored enterprises
May 15	A year's annual appropriations may be con-sidered in the House in absence of a budget resolution
June 10	House Appropriations Committee reports last annual appropriations bill
June 30	House completes action on annual appropriations bills
Prior to July 1	The President must order a sequester within 15 days of enactment of appropriations that exceed a fiscal year's caps; if appropriations are enacted after July 1 that exceed that year's caps, the caps for the next fiscal year are lowered
July 15	President submits mid-session budget review to Congress
August 10	Presidential notification regarding exempting military personnel from sequestration
August 15	CBO submits the sequestration update report
August 20	OMB submits the sequestration update report
No later than September 15	Committees of jurisdiction in the House shall report shall report legislation to the House to ensure the financial soundness of government-sponsored enterprises
October 1	Fiscal year begins
October 4	Target adjournment date

The 112th Congress and the year 2012 ended with continued disagreement between the White House and Capitol Hill over the make-up and size of the federal government's budget. The potential catastrophe of the "fiscal cliff" was postponed for two months. Again, disagreement between the conservatives in Congress and the Obama administration on automatic spending cuts and the nation's debt ceiling remain at the heart of the dispute.

NOTES

Lobbying on Capitol Hill

Most Americans outside of Washington believe that a lobbyist's main work in life is to influence members of Congress with money, fancy parties and expensive trips. Very few people realize that lobbying, or influencing legislation, is very much tied to the First Amendment of the Constitution, the right to free speech.

As a result there is little regulation of lobbying activities. Congress did pass a law in 1946 requiring lobbyists to register with the clerk of the House and the secretary of the Senate and to report the money spent on lobbying activities on a quarterly basis. However, a Supreme Court ruling in 1954 weakened the law, and any efforts toward further regulation or reform have gone nowhere for fear of obstructing citizens' access to their elected officials.

James Madison and the other founding fathers who wrote the Constitution over 200 years ago would not be surprised by the presence of the thousands of lobbyists in the nation's capital. The system of government they designed allows conflicting perspectives to be aired. In fact, Madison wrote, "Liberty is to faction [group] what air is to fire." It was believed that the presence of competing factions would be healthy for the Republic.

lobbyists
One story states that the term originated at the Willard Hotel in Washington, DC, where it was used by Ulysses S. Grant to describe the political wheelers and dealers who frequented the hotel's lobby to access Grant—who was often there to enjoy a cigar and brandy.

The term "lobbyist" came into common parlance in Washington by the 1830s. Depicted by political cartoonists as sinister, cigar-smoking, money-grubbing individuals, lobbyists were not highly regarded. Prestigious individuals in the 1830s, such as Daniel Webster, and many of the senators in the Gilded Age of the 1870s and 1880s often voted in favor of the interests of the bankers and the magnates of the steel, oil and railroad industries.

What must be kept in mind, however, is that the United States has a government that responds to the presence and pressure of interest groups. Whether abolitionists in the nineteenth century who opposed slavery, anti-saloon leaguers who led the drive for prohibition in the early twentieth century, anti-Vietnam war protestors and environmentalists of the 1960s and 1970s or pro-life or anti-gun activists in the 21st century, all of these "special interest" groups have been able to petition Congress for their causes because of our form of government.

Currently, there are more than 366,000 registered lobbyists in Washington. Most of them believe that their purpose is to inform and to educate the members of Congress, their staffs and the bureaucrats in the executive branch agencies in an effort to influence policy-making. The presentation of information cannot be stressed enough. If inaccurate or false information is given out, making a representative or a senator look foolish in public, all access to the member's office is usually ended and the organization's credibility is tainted.

Lobbyists represent businesses (e.g., Chamber of Commerce), state and local government (e.g., National Governors' Association), corporations (e.g., General Motors, IBM and Microsoft), and foreign governments and businesses (e.g., Patton/Boggs Associates, Inc.). Statistics have shown that 65 percent of Americans belong to at least one group, ranging from church-affiliated organizations to labor unions to service clubs to nationality organizations. Alexis de Tocqueville observed this "groupiness" in the country as long ago as 1825 when he wrote that Americans of all "conditions, minds, and ages, daily acquire a general taste for association and grow accustomed to the use of it." More than 5,000 organizations, or groups, are represented in Washington today.

Obviously, some of these groups are more powerful than others. But this is not to suggest that the smaller, less-monied organizations are unable to unite against the "big boys." Building coalitions of interest groups to either promote or defeat legislation has become one of the most effective lobbying techniques in recent years. Much of this kind of work takes place off Capitol Hill in offices around town. The issues are defined and strategies mapped out among the various organizations involved, although allies on one issue may well be opponents on another. Environmental legislation in recent years has seen a coalition of big industry and labor united against environmentalists and health groups. Broad-based coalitions also make the task of lobbying easier on Capitol Hill where a growing number of committees and subcommittees since the early 1970s has greatly increased the burden of the lobbyist.

Direct access to a representative or a senator is desired by many, but most contact on the Hill occurs between the lobbyist and congressional staff. Knowing the interests of a member's personal staff and how the office works as well as the profile of the state or district enhance an organization's ability "to get through the door."

Having obtained access, the association, corporation or foreign government is now in the position to argue its case for or against legislation by presenting succinct and accurate information. Lobbying groups are often viewed as the issue experts in their areas. Often they are more knowledgeable about the technicalities of the legislation than the elected officials, their staffs or a federal agency. Indeed, supported by their own staffs of lawyers and legislative experts, interest groups are frequently called on to testify before committees, to help write legislation, and to draft amendments in committee markup sessions. The more knowledgeable an organization and the greater its reputation, the more likely its input will be requested at hearings.

Prior to the early 1970s, committee hearings, markup sessions and conference committees were not open. For the most part, all of these sessions are open today thus allowing for greater input in more places. Access to conference committees has been limited since the mid-1990s.

In recent years, allegiance to and appreciation of the power of the elected official's constituency have grown. Since members of Congress are sensitive to local feelings, grass-roots lobbying has increased. The ability to generate letters on an issue, to organize timely and effective local visits to a hospital or a weapons factory and to encourage newspapers across the district or state to write editorials is a skill developed by lobbying groups based in Washington.

Modern communications and high tech have had a tremendous impact on the political process; computers can help generate mass mailings of postcards to all offices on Capitol Hill. Since 1980, mass-mailing techniques as well as faxing and the use of electronic mail via computer have been used by lobbyists to affect legislation. Although the high-tech generated mail still does not have the effect on elected officials that personal letters from constituents have, thousands of postcards sent on a single issue reflect some kind of interest back home.

Lobbying groups also generate grass-roots support or opposition to a particular issue through radio, television, magazines and op-ed pieces in local newspapers. Often full-page ads are run by interest groups in major newspapers; a favorite is *The Washington Post* to which just about all of the 541 members of Congress subscribe.

In 1996 Congress passed and President Clinton signed into law "The Lobby Disclosure Act of 1996." It was an effort to close loopholes in existing lobbying regulation laws. Some of these provisions included limits on lobbying policy-making officials in the executive branch. Reports of who lobbies which agencies of the executive branch and which houses of Congress in addition to the issues lobbied must be made. And, finally, anyone who spends less than 20 percent of their time lobbying is exempted from this legislation.

Even with these efforts at lobbying reform, some members of the 21st century Washington lobbying community pushed the law to the limit. Jack Abrahamhoff and his associates, who included former staff of high-level congressional leaders, have been indicted. The investigations may lead to more lobbying reforms. However, without further campaign finance reform the behavior of lobbyists may continue.

Finally, a very important lobbying technique is that of campaign financial support. Running for Congress has become an expensive process: the average House race costs nearly $3.5 million, a Senate race over $7 million. Incumbents and challengers are accepting money increasingly from the political action committees (PACs) of interest groups. A PAC is a campaign fund sponsored by a corporation, a labor union, a non-profit or other outside entity. Its purpose is to contribute to the campaigns of those running for federal office. The limit of PAC contributions is $15,000 for each election cycle with three races, the primary, the runoff, if necessary, and the general election.

By contributing to a candidate's campaign it is hoped that easier access to the official would be possible and that support for the group's cause would be obtained. Such a system favors the incumbent who already has name recognition and who the organization wants to keep in office if he or she supports its position.

PACs are legal and have been around in other forms for some years. They have been subject to much criticism and have generated the fear that elected officials will become more loyal to the interests contributing to their campaign than to the interests of the district or state. Voter disinterest in the political process has contributed to this fear.

In an effort to control campaign spending in 2002 Congress passed and President George W. Bush signed in to law the Bipartisan Campaign Reform Act (BCRA), also known as McCain Feingold, the Senate sponsors of the bill. Essentially, the bill banned soft money, the huge unlimited donations from corporations, wealthy individuals and labor unions. Challenged by its opponents as a limit to free speech, the

Supreme Court ruled in favor of BCRA in December of 2003.

In January of 2010 the Supreme Court ruling on the case, *Citizens United v. the Federal Election Commission*, overruled McCain-Feingold. Arguing that the government could not deny the political spending of corporations, labor unions and other outside groups, the Supreme Court declared that campaign monetary contributions are a form of free speech. The dissenters, led by John Paul Stevens, wrote that corporate contributions (speech) should not be given the same status as human speech. Progressive, liberal groups expressed initial concerns that a flood of corporate money (this applies to labor unions as well) could affect the way elections are conducted.

Some would argue that such a concern proved to be valid for the 2010 midterm elections. Following the Citizens United ruling outside groups, ranging from Fortune 500 companies to small businesses to labor unions, created "super PACS," officially known as "independent expenditure only committees." These entities may now engage in unlimited, anonymous campaign contributions to political candidates.

Opensecrets.org, a web site created by the Center for Responsive Politics in Washington, DC, tracked the contributions and expenditures for all races in 2010 but especially for those for House and Senate seats. Nearly $1 billion was raised for congressional races. Of that amount over half or $551 million came from individuals and the "super PACS." Donations from PACS are still limited to $5000 for each race, whether primary or general election.

As of the writing of this edition of the book in late 2010 nearly 10 million Americans are out of work with many more millions under-employed or employed part-time. How many people could have been employed, with benefits, for $1 billion dollars in 2010?

Exercise: Researching Lobbyists

Go to **house.gov**.

Click on the link on the left for **Clerk of the House**.

On the second menu bar below the picture in the middle of the page, click on **LOBBYING DISCLOSURE**.

On the left side of the page, click on **Lobby Disclosure Filing Search** below the Public Disclosure Search heading.

Select **Client State** from the drop down menus next to the first Search Field. In the Criteria column, a drop down menu with all of the states will appear. **Choose your state**.

Leave the sort options as they are and click the **Search** button.

All of the lobbyists groups associated with the state you chose will appear.

Notes

NOTES

GETTING AROUND ON CAPITOL HILL

Knowledge and understanding of the legislative process are crucial to gain an insight into Congress. It is often recommended that proceedings be observed and meetings held with staff and elected officials on Capitol Hill.

This chapter covers the physical layout of "the Hill," useful information regarding Hill security, and entrances to buildings for visitors, especially those who are physically disabled. It also contains suggestions for attendance at committee hearings and House and Senate floor proceedings, and an explanation of bell codes for House and Senate floor activity.

TRANSPORTATION TO CAPITOL HILL

Although Congress is one of the most open legislative bodies in the world, there is limited parking for the public, even more so since the attacks of 9/11. Meters are scarce and towing is strictly enforced. Public garages are a long walk from offices, and are expensive. There is public parking at Union Station on the Senate side of Capitol Hill. Those who go to the Hill on a regular basis use either taxis or Washington's subway system, called the Metro. For most visitors, the Metro is the best means of transportation.

Metro Subway System

Dark-brown pylons with a large white "M" indicate the Metro station entrances. The two stations closest to Capitol Hill are the Capitol South Station (Blue and Orange Lines) on the House side of the Hill at First and C Sts., SE and Union Station (Red Line) on the Senate side.

Fares for Metro differ according to distances traveled and time of day (i.e., rush-hour fares cost more than non-rush hour fares). Fares can be determined easily by consulting the route and fare maps posted at all Metro stations.

Washington's subway system is perhaps the most convenient, relatively hassle free mode of traveling about the city and is highly recommended. Trains operate 5:00 a.m. to midnight during the week and 7 a.m. to 3 a.m. on the weekend. The schedule differs on holidays. To obtain schedule information call (202) 637-7000, 6 a.m. to 11:30 p.m.

HOUSE AND SENATE OFFICE BUILDINGS
House Office Buildings

The map on the following page gives an aerial view of the layout of Capitol Hill. The office buildings of the House of Representatives are found along Independence Avenue. In descending order from that closest to the Capitol South Metro Station are the Cannon, Longworth, and Rayburn House Office Buildings. The offices of the 441 members of the House of Representatives and their staffs are housed in these buildings. Closest to the Capitol Souther Metro stop are visitors entrances to each of these buildings located on C St., SE. House committees and their staffs also have offices there as well as in the House side of the Capitol. The map shows the Ford House Office Building, which also contains staff offices. Street addresses and room numbering systems follow:

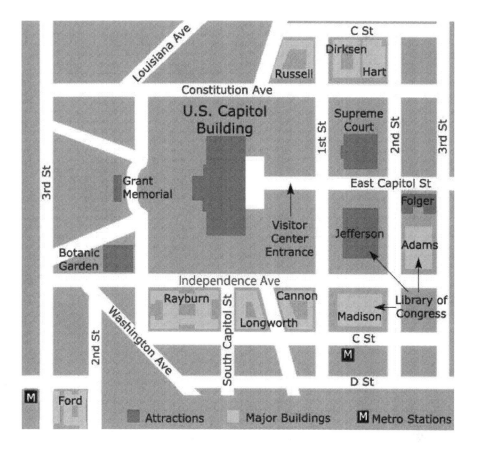

Cannon House Office Building (CHOB)

Independence Ave. and 1st St., S.E. (Room numbers have three digits; first digit is the floor number, i.e. 312 is on the third floor.)

Longworth House Office Building (LHOB)

Independence Ave. and New Jersey Ave., S.E. (Room numbers have four digits; second digit is the floor number, i.e., Room 1412 is on the fourth floor.)

Rayburn House Office Building (RHOB)

Independence Ave. between 1st St., S.W. and South Capitol St., S.W. (Room numbers have four digits, second digit is the floor number, i.e., Room 2502 is on the fifth floor.)

Ford House Office Building (formerly Annex II)

2nd and D Streets, S.E.

Senate Office Buildings

The Senate office buildings are located along Constitution Avenue. These buildings also contain the senators' and their staffs' offices as well as Senate committee offices. Several Senate committee offices are also located in the Senate side of the Capitol. The street addresses and room numbering systems of the Senate office buildings follow:

HSOB - Hart Senate Office Building (HSOB)

Constitution Ave. and 2nd St., N.E. (Room numbers have three digits; first digit is the floor number)

DSOB - Dirksen Senate Office Building (DSOB)

Constitution Ave. and 1st St., N.E. (Room numbers have three digits; the first digit is the floor number)

RSOB - Russell Senate Office Building (RSOB)

Constitution Ave. and Delaware Ave., N.E. (Room numbers have three digits; the first digit is the floor number)

SECURITY

Since the terrorist attack on Washington in September, 2001, access to the Capitol and office buildings has meant that visitors can enter buildings only through designated entrances. The previous map indicates visitors' entrances. Quite similar to airport security, the Capitol police -- located at these designated places - inspect packages, bags, and purses before each person passes through a metal detector. All buildings prohibit any kind of gun, knife, box cutter, or pepper spray. For access to the U.S. Capitol building, the Capitol Hill Police has also forbidden any bags larger than 13" x 14" x 4", any bottles, cans, or food.

VISITORS' ACCESS TO THE HOUSE AND SENATE OFFICE BUILDINGS

Once inside the House and Senate office buildings, the visitor is free to visit member and staff offices, attend open committee sessions. In periods of inclement weather or for access to other buildings, visitors can use a series of tunnels that connect the House and Senate office buildings. The Capitol police will assist anyone in need of direction.

ACCESS FOR THE PHYSICALLY DISABLED

All street intersections on Capitol Hill have low, ramp-like curbs and all buildings have facilities to accommodate the physically disabled. Building guards know the location of these facilities, which include ramps, special elevators, telephones, and restrooms.

The map on p. 111 indicates those entrances where access ramps or other arrangements have been constructed to accommodate the needs of people using wheelchairs.

ACCESS TO THE U.S. CAPITOL AND TOURS

There is no general public entrance to the Capitol building. To enter the U.S. Capitol building, there are only three following choices:

1. Information concerning tours of the Capitol as well as s tour arrangements may be obtained either through your representative or senators' offices or through the Capitol Visitor Center (CVC) whose web site is visitthecapitol.gov:

2. A congressional staff member may conduct tours;

3. Ask you representative or senators' offices to provide your desired visiting information to the Sergeant at Arms office which will enable you to enter via the North or South security desks.

Security for the U.S. Capitol building is very much like airport security. *No liquids or food are allowed*.

PHYSICALLY DISABLED ACCESS TO HOUSE AND SENATE OFFICE BUILDINGS
House Office Buildings
Rayburn Building

The "horseshoe entrance" on South Capitol Street has an access ramp from the driveway promenade in front of the doors to the building. It is also possible to gain access to this building at the Independence Avenue entrance to this building.

Longworth Building

The Longworth Building has first floor access at Independence Avenue. The tunnel to the Cannon Building is on the B-level.

The Cannon Building

This building has a ramp at the New Jersey Avenue entrance. The revolving doors can be pushed to one side to allow for wheelchair access.

Senate Office Buildings
Hart Building

The Hart Building may be accessed by using the ramp at the front of the building on Constitution Avenue. There is no ramp on the C Street, N.E., side of the building. Corridors, doors, and elevators have been constructed to accommodate wheelchairs. All restrooms are accessible. The Hart Building and the Dirksen Building are contiguous on each floor, so that those in wheelchairs can pass conveniently from one floor to the other.

The House Chamber

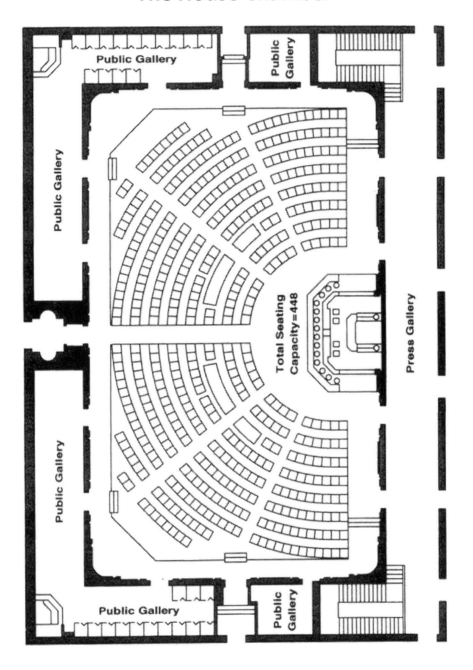

The Senate Chamber

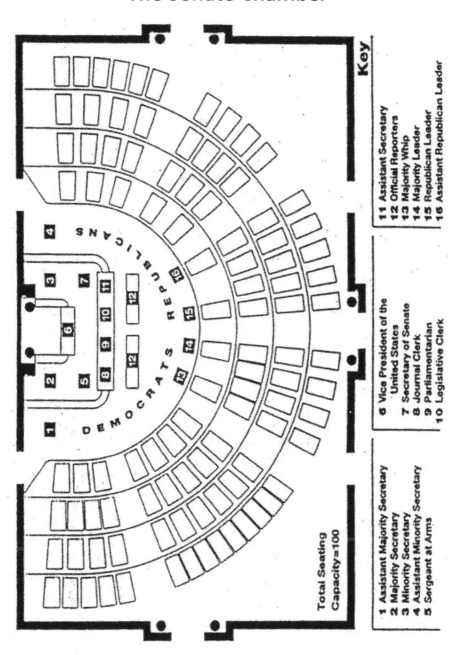

Key

1 Assistant Majority Secretary
2 Majority Secretary
3 Minority Secretary
4 Assistant Minority Secretary
5 Sergeant at Arms

6 Vice President of the United States
7 Secretary of Senate
8 Journal Clerk
9 Parliamentarian
10 Legislative Clerk

11 Assistant Secretary
12 Official Reporters
13 Majority Whip
14 Majority Leader
15 Republican Leader
16 Assistant Republican Leader

Total Seating Capacity=100

Dirksen Building

On the ground level, access to Dirksen is on the C Street, N.E., side of the building. Elevators are small but will accommodate wheelchairs. Restrooms on the first and fourth floors are accessible.

Russell Building

A ramp is located on the Delaware Avenue side of the building. Some restrooms are equipped for the physically disabled. Ask the guards for their locations.

ATTENDANCE AT CONGRESSIONAL COMMITTEE HEARINGS

Congressional committee hearings take place in the House and Senate offices buildings as well as in the U.S. Capitol. Go to woodsinstitute.com and click on the link on the left side of the home page to go to links that list the Hearing Schedule for both the House and Senate Unless indicated to the contrary, hearings are open to the public and require no pass for entry.

When Congress is in session, most committee hearings take place on Tuesday, Wednesday, and Thursday.

ATTENDANCE AT THE HOUSE AND SENATE GALLERIES

A visitor must obtain gallery passes to observe floor proceedings in the House and Senate. (See proceeding pages for a layout of each of these chambers.) These passes may be obtained from the visitor's representative and senators' offices. After obtaining your passes, you enter the Capitol building through the CVC. No electronic devices are permitted in the House and Senate galleries. Items such as pagers, cell phones, laptops, may be checked at secured points on either the House or Senate side of the CVC.

For scheduling House or Senate floor information, www.clerk.house. gov or www.clerk.senate.gov provide good guides. For minute by minute House and Senate floor information, the current phone number for the House is 202-225-7430; for the Senate the number is 202-224-8541.

HOUSE AND SENATE FLOOR ACTION

For representatives and senators to keep up to the minute on floor activity when the House and Senate are in session, a series of lights and bells can be seen and heard in all of the office buildings and the Capitol to alert the elected officials to specific activities. Explanations of their meaning are presented on the following pages.

LEGISLATIVE BELLS AND SIGNALS
U.S. Senate

One long ring at hour of convening. One red light remains lit while the Senate is in session. Where lights exist, they will correspond with the following rings:

1 ring: Yeas and nays.

2 rings: Quorum call.

3 rings: Call of absentees.

4 rings: Adjournment or recess.

5 rings: Seven and a half minutes remaining on yea and nay vote.

6 rings: Morning business concluded.

U.S. House of Representatives

1 ring and light: Tellers (not a recorded vote).

1 long ring and light (pause) followed by 3 rings and lights: Signals the start or continuation of a notice of a quorum call.

1 long ring and light: Termination of a notice of a quorum call.

2 rings and lights: Electronically recorded vote.

2 rings and lights (pause) followed by 2 rings and lights: Manual roll call vote and the rings will be sounded again when the clerk reaches the R's.

2 rings and lights (pause) followed by 5 bells: First vote under suspension of the rules or on clustered votes (2 rings will be rung 5 minutes later). The first vote will take 15 minutes with successive votes at intervals of not less than 5 minutes. Each successive vote will be signaled by 5 rings.

3 rings and lights: Quorum call, either initially or after a notice of quorum has been converted to a regular quorum. The rings are repeated 5 minutes after the first ring.

3 rings and lights (pause) followed by 3 rings and lights: Manual quorum call. The rings will be sounded again when the clerk reaches the R's.

3 rings and lights (pause) followed by 5 rings: Quorum call in the committee of the whole, which may be followed by a 5-minute recorded vote.

4 rings and lights: Adjournment of the House.

5 rings and lights: Five-minute electronically recorded vote.

6 rings and lights: Recess of the House.

NOTES

NOTES

APPENDIX A
COMMITTEES IN THE UNITED STATES SENATE

Committee on Agriculture, Nutrition and Forestry
328A Senate Russell Office Building
Washington, DC 20510
202-224-2035
ag.senate.gov

This committee has jurisdiction over legislation in areas such as agriculture, economics and research; production, marketing, and price supports; crop insurance and farm security; food stamps; forestry and wilderness not in the public domain; inspection of meat and livestock; international food programs; and rural development and electrification. Its subcommittees include: Forestry, Conservation, and Rural Revitalization; Marketing, Inspection, and Product Promotion; Production and Price Competitiveness; and Research, Nutrition, and General Legislation.

Committee on Appropriations
The Capitol
Room S 128
Washington, DC 20510
Telephone 202-224-7363
appropriations.senate.gov

This committee has jurisdiction over legislation related to revenue appropriated for the support of the U.S. government; rescission of appropriated funds; and the new spending authority described in the Congressional Budget Act of 1974 as part of the budget process. Its subcommittees include: Agriculture, Rural Development, and Related Agencies; Commerce, Justice, and Science; Defense; District of Columbia; Energy and Water Development; Homeland Security; Interior and Related Agencies; Labor, Health and Human Services, Education, and Related Agencies; Legislative Branch; Military Construction and Veterans' Affairs; Transportation, State, Foreign Operations, and Related Agencies; and Treasury, the Judiciary, Housing and Urban Development (HUD) and Independent Agencies.

Committee on Armed Services
Room SR-228, Russell Senate Office Building
Washington, DC 20510-6050
202-224-3871
armed-services.senate.gov

This committee has jurisdiction over legislation in areas such as aeronautical and space activities related to weapons systems or military operations; the common defense; the Departments of Defense, Army, Navy, and Air Force; the Strategic Defense Initiative; national security aspects of nuclear energy; and Naval petroleum reserves (not Alaska). Its subcommittees include: AirLand Forces; Acquisition and Technology; Personnel; Readiness; Seapower and Strategic Forces.

Committee on Banking, Housing and Urban Affairs
534 Dirksen Senate Office Building
Washington, DC 20510
(202) 224-7391
banking.senate.gov

This committee has jurisdiction over legislation in areas such as banks and financial institutions; control of price commodities; rents and services; deposit insurance; export and foreign trade promotion; federal monetary policy; nursing home construction; public and private housing; and urban development and mass transit. Its subcommittees include: Financial Institutions and Regulatory Relief; Financial Services and Technology; Housing Opportunity and Community Development; International Finance; and Securities.

Committee on the Budget
624 Dirksen Senate Office Building
Washington, DC 20510
(202) 224-0642
banking.senate.gov

This committee drafts the concurrent budget resolution in accordance with the Balanced Budget and Emergency Deficit Control Act of 1985. It also makes studies on the effect of budget outlays of relevant existing and proposed legislation, and it requests and evaluates continuing studies of tax expenditures, policies, and programs. This committee has no subcommittees.

Committee on Commerce, Science and Transportation
Dirksen 508
Washington, DC 20510
202-224-0411
commerce.senate.gov

This committee has jurisdiction over legislation in areas such as the Coast Guard; coastal zone management; communications; highway safety; marine fisheries and merchant marine; nonmilitary space sciences; regulation of consumer products (including testing of toxic substances); sports; and transportation. Its subcommittees include: Aviation; Communications; Consumer Affairs, Foreign Commerce, and Tourism; Manufacturing and Competitiveness; Oceans and Fisheries; Science, Technology, and Space; and Surface Transportation and Merchant Marine.

Committee on Energy and Natural Resources
304 Dirksen Senate Building
Washington, DC 20510
224-4971
energy.senate.gov

This committee has jurisdiction over legislation in areas such as coal production; energy policy and regulation; extraction of minerals from areas and outer continental shelf lands; hydroelectric power; national parks; recreation and wilderness areas; oil and gas production and distribution; public lands and forests; and solar energy. Its subcommittees include: Energy Research, Production, Development, and Regulation; Forests and Public Land Management; Parks, Historic Preservation, and Recreation; and Water and Power.

Committee on Environment and Public Works
410 Dirksen Senate Office Bldg.
Washington, DC 20510-6175
224-8832
epw.senate.gov

This committee has jurisdiction over legislation in areas such as air pollution; construction and maintenance of highways; environmental effects of toxic substances (not pesticides); fisheries and wildlife; ocean dumping; public works, bridges, and dams; solid waste disposal; and water pollution. Its subcommittees include: Clean Air, Wetlands, Private Property, and Nuclear Safety; Drinking Water, Fisheries, and Wildlife; Superfund, Waste Control, and Risk Assessment; and Transportation and Infrastructure.

Committee on Finance
219 Dirksen Senate Office Building
Washington, DC 20510
224-5315
finance.senate.gov

This committee has jurisdiction over legislation in areas such as the bonded debt of the U.S. government; customs and ports of entry; deposit of public monies; health programs under the Social Security Act; reciprocal trade agreements; and revenue (tax) measures generally. Its subcommittees include: Health Care; International Trade; Long Term Growth, Debt and Deficit Reduction; Social Security and Family Policy; and Taxation and IRS Oversight.

Committee on Foreign Relations
446 Dirksen Senate Office Building
Washington, DC 20510
224-4651
foreign.senate.gov

This committee has jurisdiction over legislation in areas such as land and buildings for U.S. embassies in foreign countries; boundaries of the United States; diplomatic service; foreign economic, military, and humanitarian assistance; International Monetary Fund; foreign loans; national security; treaties; and declarations of war. Its subcommittees include: African Affairs; East Asian and Pacific Affairs; European Affairs; International Economic Policy, Export, and Trade Promotion; International Operations; Near Eastern and South Asian Affairs; and Western Hemisphere, Peace Corps, Narcotics, and Terrorism.

Committee on Health, Education, Labor and Pensions
428 Senate Dirksen Office Building
Washington, DC 20510
224-5375
help.senate.gov

This committee has jurisdiction over legislation in areas such as education, labor, health, and public welfare; aging; agricultural colleges; arts and humanities; biomedical research and development; child labor; convict labor; equal employment opportunity; Gallaudet College, Howard University, and St. Elizabeth's Hospital; the handicapped; labor standards; private pension plans; public health; student loans; and wages and hours of labor. Its subcommittees include: Children and families; Employment and Workplace Safety; and Retirement and Aging.

Committee on Homeland Security and Governmental Affairs
340 Dirksen Senate Office Building
Washington, DC 20510
224-2627
hsgac.senate.gov

This committee has jurisdiction over legislation in areas such as the National Archives; census and collection of statistics; congressional organizations such as the General Accounting Office and the Congressional Research Service; District of Columbia; the Department of Homeland Security; intergovernmental relations; nuclear export policy; and postal service. Its subcommittees include: International Security, Proliferation, and Federal Services; Oversight of Government Management, Restructuring, and the District of Columbia; and Permanent Subcommittee on Investigations.

Committee on the Judiciary
224-7703
judiciary.senate.gov

This committee has jurisdiction over legislation in areas such as apportionment of representatives; bankruptcy, mutiny, espionage, and counterfeiting; civil liberties; constitutional amendments; federal courts and judges; judicial proceedings, civil and criminal; immigration and naturalization; patents, copy rights, and trademarks; protection of trade against monopolies; and state and territorial boundary lines. Its subcommittees include: Administrative Oversight and the Courts; Antitrust, Business Rights, and Competition; Constitution, Federalism, and Property Rights; Immigration; Terrorism, Technology, and Government Information; and Youth Violence.

Committee on Rules and Administration
305 Russell Senate Office Building
Washington, DC 20510
224-6352
rules.senate.gov

This committee has jurisdiction over legislation in areas such as the administration of Senate office buildings and the Senate wing of the U.S. Capitol; Senate rules and regulations; corrupt practices; credentials and qualifications of members of the Senate; federal elections, including the election of the President, vice president, and members of the Congress; the Government Printing Office; presidential succession; and public buildings such as the Library of Congress, the Smithsonian Institution, and the Botanic Garden. This committee has no subcommittees.

Committee on Small Business and Entrepreneurship
428A Russell Senate Office Bldg
Washington, DC 20510
224-5175
sbc.senate.gov

This committee has jurisdiction over legislation in areas such as the administration of the Small Business Administration; and the problems and regulation of American small business enterprise. This committee has no subcommittees.

Committee on Veterans' Affairs
412 Russell Senate Bldg.
Washington DC 20510
224-9126
veterans.senate.gov

This committee has jurisdiction over legislation in areas such as compensation of veterans; life insurance by the government on service in the Armed Forces; national cemeteries; pensions of all wars of the United States; and soldiers' and sailors' civil relief. This committee has no subcommittees.

Select Committee on Ethics
220 Hart Building
Washington, DC 20510.
224 - 2981
ethics.senate.gov

This committee administers, interprets, and enforces the Senate's Code of Official Conduct; receives complaints and investigates allegations of improper conduct; recommends disciplinary action; and recommends new rules or regulations. It receives complaints about violations of Senate mail franking privileges, issues decisions, and takes other appropriate actions to enforce franking rules. The committee also investigates allegations of unauthorized disclosure of information from the Select Committee on Intelligence. This committee has no subcommittees.

Select Committee on Intelligence
211 Hart Senate Office Building
Washington, DC 20510
224-1700
intelligence.senate.gov

This committee oversees and studies the intelligence activities and programs of the U.S. government. It submits appropriate proposals for legislation and makes reports to the Senate concerning intelligence activities and programs. It also assures that relevant departments and agencies provide the intelligence necessary for executive and legislative branches to make sound decisions concerning security and other vital national interests. The committee acts to ensure that intelligence activities conform with the Constitution and laws of the United States. This committee has no subcommittees.

Select Committee on Indian Affairs
838 Hart Office Building
Washington, DC 20510
224-2251
indian.senate.gov

This committee has jurisdiction to study the unique problems of American Indian, Native Hawaiian, and Alaska Native peoples and to propose legislation to alleviate these difficulties. These issues include, but are not limited to, Indian education, economic development, land management, trust responsibilities, health care, and claims against the United States. Additionally, all legislation proposed by members of the Senate that specifically pertains to American Indians, Native Hawaiians, or Alaska Natives is under the jurisdiction of the committee. This committee has no subcommittees.

Special Committee on Aging
G31 Dirksen Senate Office Building
Washington, DC 20510
202-224-5364
aging.senate.gov

This committee studies any and all matters pertaining to the problems and opportunities of older people, including, but not limited to, health maintenance, adequate income, employment, productive and rewarding activity, proper housing, and, when necessary, access to care or assistance. No proposed legislation is referred to the committee, and the committee cannot report by bill, or otherwise have legislative jurisdiction. It reports to the Senate, not less than once each year, the results of its studies and its recommendations. This committee has no subcommittees.

U.S. HOUSE OF REPRESENTATIVES

Committee on Agriculture
1301 Longworth House Office Building
Washington, DC 20515
225-2171
agriculture.house.gov

This committee has jurisdiction over legislation in areas such as adulteration of seeds and protection of birds and animals in forest reserves; agriculture generally; agricultural colleges and experiment stations; agricultural production, marketing, and prices; crop insurance; dairy industry; forestry in general and forest reserves other than those created from the public domain; meat and livestock inspection; rural development; human nutrition; and food inspection. Its subcommittees include: Conservation, Credit, Energy, and Research; Department Operations, Oversight, Nutrition, and Forestry; General Farm Commodities and Risk Management; Horticulture and Organic Agriculture; Livestock, Dairy, and Poultry; and, Rural Development, Biotechnology, Specialty Crops, and Foreign Agriculture.

Committee on Appropriations
H-218 U.S. Capitol
Washington D.C. 20515
225-2771
appropriations.house.gov

This committee has jurisdiction over legislation related to revenue appropriated for the support of the U.S. government; rescission of appropriated funds; and the new spending authority described in the Congressional Budget Act of 1974 as part of the budget process. Its subcommittees include: Agriculture; Commerce, Justice, Science; Defense; Energy and Water; Financial Services; Homeland Security; Interior and Environment; Labor, HHS, Education; Legislative Branch; Military Construction, VA; State, Foreign Operations; and, Transportation, HUD.

Committee on Armed Services
2120 Rayburn House Office Building
Washington, DC 20515
225-4151
armedservices.house.gov

The committee will continue its oversight and assessment of threats to U.S. national security and U.S. interests. The committee will regularly assess national security threats and challenges as it begins consideration of the fiscal year 2000 and fiscal year 2001 defense budget requests. This effort will involve appropriate oversight hearings with the secretary of defense, the chairman of the Joint Chiefs of Staff, the individual service secretaries and chiefs of staff, regional commanders-in-chief, other officials of the Department of Defense and the military departments, officials of the Central Intelligence Agency and other defense-related intelligence agencies, and officials of the Department of Energy. In addition, the committee will invite the views and perspectives of outside experts in academia, industry, associations, and those in private life on these matters. Its subcommittees include: Air and Land Forces; Defense Acquisition Reform Panel; Military Personnel; Oversight and Investigations; Readiness; Seapower and Expeditionary Forces; Strategic Forces; and, Terrorism, Unconventional Threats and Capabilities.

Committee on the Budget
207 Cannon House Office Building
Washington, DC 20515
226-7200
budget.house.gov

This committee drafts the concurrent budget resolution in accordance with the Balanced Budget and Emergency Deficit Control Act of 1985. It also makes studies on the effect of budget outlays of relevant, existing, and proposed legislation, and it requests and evaluates continuing studies of tax expenditures, policies, and programs. This committee has no subcommittees.

Committee on Education and Workforce
2181 Rayburn House Office Building
Washington, DC 20515
225-3725 (D)
edlabor.house.gov

This committee has jurisdiction over legislation in areas such as measures relating to education and labor generally; child labor; convict labor; labor standards and statistics; mediation and arbitration of labor disputes; food programs for school children; vocational rehabilitation; wages and hours of labor; and welfare of minors. Its subcommittees include: Early Childhood, Youth, and Families; Employer-Employee Relations; Oversight and Investigations; Postsecondary Education, Training, and Lifelong Learning; and, Workforce Protections.

Committee on Energy and Commerce
2125 Rayburn House Office Building
Washington, DC 20515
225-2927
energycommerce.house.gov

This committee has jurisdiction over legislation in areas such as interstate and foreign commerce generally; national energy policy and energy information; measures relating to the exploration, production, storage, supply, marketing, pricing, and regulation of all fossil fuels and solar energy; conservation of energy resources; interstate energy compacts; and travel and tourism. Its subcommittees include: Commerce, Trade, and Consumer Protection; Communications, Technology, and the Internet; Energy and Environment; Health; and, Oversight and Investigations.

Committee on Financial Services
2129 Rayburn House Office Building
Washington, DC 20515
225-4247
financialservices.house.gov

This committee has jurisdiction over legislation in areas such as banks and banking, including deposit insurance, federal monetary policy and has primary jurisdiction over the Glass-Steagall Act, which governs security activities of banks; money and credit, including currency and notes; urban development; private and public housing; international finance; and international financial and monetary organizations. Its subcommittees include: Capital Markets; Financial Institutions & Consumer Credit; Housing & Community Opportunity; Domestic Monetary Policy & Technology; International Monetary Policy & Trade; and, Oversight & Investigations.

Committee on Foreign Affairs
2170 Rayburn House Office Building
Washington, DC 20515
225-5021
foreignaffairs.house.gov

This committee has jurisdiction over legislation in areas such as relations between the United States and foreign nations generally; acquisition of land and buildings for embassies in foreign countries; U.S. boundaries; foreign loans; intervention abroad and declarations of war; diplomatic service; American Red Cross; United Nations' organizations; and international education. Its subcommittees include: Africa and Global Health; Asia, the Pacific and the Global Environment; Europe; Terrorism, Nonproliferation and Trade; International Organizations, Human Rights and Oversight; Middle East and South Asia; and, Western Hemisphere.

Committee on Homeland Security
176 Ford House Office Building
Washington, DC 20515
225-2616
hsc.house.gov

This committee has jurisdiction on overall homeland security policy; organization and administration and function of the Department of Homeland Security; border and port security (except immigration policy and non-border enforcement); customs (except customs revenue); integration, analysis, and dissemination of homeland security information; domestic preparedness for and collective response to terrorism; research and development; transportation security. Its subcommittees include: Border, Maritime and Global Counterterrorism; Intelligence, Information Sharing and Terrorism Risk Assessment; Transportation Security and Infrastructure Protection; Emerging Threats, Cybersecurity, and Science and Technology; Emergency Communications, Preparedness, and Response; and, Management, Investigations, and Oversight.

Committee on House Administration
1309 Longworth Building
Washington, DC 20515
225-2061
cha.house.gov

This committee has jurisdiction over legislation in areas including employment of persons by the House such as clerks for committees and reporters for debates; matters relating to the Library of Congress, the Botanic Garden, and the House Library; matters relating to the printing and correction of the Congressional Record; assignment of office space for House members; House members' campaign funds; and House members' retirement. This committee has no subcommittees.

Committee on Oversight and Government Reform
2157 Rayburn House Office Building
Washington, DC 20515
225-5051
oversight.house.gov

This committee has jurisdiction over legislation in areas such as budget and accounting measures other than budget and appropriations; reorganization of the executive branch of government; intergovernmental relations; national archives; and overall economy and efficiency of government operations and activities, including federal procurement. Its subcommittees include: Domestic Policy; Federal Workforce, Postal Service and the District of Columbia; Government Management, Organization, and Procurement; Information Policy, Census and National Archives; and, National Security and Foreign Affairs.

Committee on the Judiciary
2138 Rayburn House Office Building
Washington, DC 20515225-3951
judiciary.house.gov

This committee has jurisdiction over legislation in areas such as judicial proceedings, civil and criminal generally; apportionment of representatives; bankruptcy, mutiny, espionage, and counterfeiting; civil liberties; constitutional amendments; federal courts and judges; immigration and naturalization; suits against the United States; patent office; presidential succession; codification of the statutes of the United States; and communist and other subversive activities affecting the internal security of the United States. Its subcommittees include: Courts and Competition Policy; Constitution, Civil Rights and Civil Liberties; Commercial and Administrative Law; Crime, Terrorism, and Homeland Security; Immigration, Citizenship, Refugees, Border Security and International Law; and Judicial Impeachment.

Committee on Natural Resources
1324 Longworth Building
Washington, DC 20515
225-6065
resources.house.gov

This committee has jurisdiction over legislation in areas such as forest reserves and national parks created from the public domain; Geological Survey; interstate compacts for irrigation purposes; Indian affairs; the insular possessions of the United States; military parks and battlefields; mining interests generally; petroleum conservation on the public lands; regulation of domestic nuclear energy; fisheries and endangered species; and the Trans-Alaska pipeline. Its subcommittees include: Energy and Mineral Resources; Insular Affairs, Oceand and Wildlife; National Parks, Forests and Public Lands; Office of Indian Affairs; and, Water and Power Resources.

Committee on Rules
H-312 The Capitol
Washington, DC 20515
225-9091
rules.house.gov

This committee has jurisdiction over legislation in areas such as the rules and joint rules (excluding ethics), and order of business of the House; emergency waivers (under the Budget Act of 1985) of the required reporting date for bills and resolutions authorizing new budget authority; and recesses and final adjournment. Its subcommittees include: Legislative and Budget Process and Rules and Organization of the House.

Committee on Science, Space and Technology
2321 Rayburn Building
Washington, DC 20515
225-6375
science.house.gov

This committee has jurisdiction over legislation in areas such as astronautical and energy research and development; NASA; National Science Foundation; outer space, including exploration and control thereof; scientific research and development in federally owned nonmilitary energy laboratories; civil aviation; and National Weather Service. Its subcommittees include: Technology and Innovation; Energy and Environment; Investigations and Oversight; Research and Science Education; and, Space and Aeronautics.

Committee on Small Business
2361 Rayburn House Office Building
Washington, DC 20515
225-4038
house.gov/smbiz

This committee has jurisdiction over legislation in areas such as assistance to and protection of small business, including financial aid; and participation of small business enterprises in federal procurement and government contracts. Its subcommittees include: Finance and Tax; Contracting and Technology; Regulations and Healthcare; Rural Development, Entrepreneurship and Trade; and, Investigations and Oversight.

Committee on Ethics
HT-2, The Capitol
Washington, DC 20515
225-7103
ethics.house.gov

This committee has jurisdiction over legislation in areas relating to the Code of Official Conduct. This committee has no subcommittees.

Committee on Transportation and Infrastructure
2165 Rayburn House Building
Washington, DC 20515
225-4472
transportation.house.gov

This committee has jurisdiction over legislation in areas such as flood control and improvement of rivers and harbors; measures relating to all of the buildings on Capitol Hill as well as the Botanic Garden, the Library of Congress, and the Smithsonian; government buildings in the District of Columbia; oil and other pollution of navigable waters; public buildings and grounds in the United States generally; water power; roads and safety thereof; railroad and inland waterways transportation; U.S. Coast Guard; and measures relating to transportation regulation agencies including the Federal Railroad Administration and Amtrak. Its subcommittees include: Aviation; Coast Guard and Maritime Transportation; Economic Development, Public Buildings, and Emergency Management; Highways and Transit; Railroads, Pipelines, and Hazardous Materials; and, Water Resources.

Committee on Veterans' Affairs
335 Cannon House Office Building
Washington, DC
225-9756
veterans.house.gov

This committee has jurisdiction over legislation in areas such as compensation of veterans; life insurance by the government on service in the Armed Forces; national cemeteries; pensions of all wars of the United States; and soldiers' and sailors' civil relief. Its subcommittees include: Disability Assistance and Memorial Affairs; Economic Opportunity; Health; and, Oversight and Investigation.

Committee on Ways and Means
1102 Longworth House Office Building
Washington, DC 20515
225-3625
waysandmeans.house.gov

This committee has jurisdiction over legislation in areas such as customs, collection districts, and ports of entry; reciprocal trade agreements; revenue (tax) measures generally and to insular possessions; the bonded debt of the United States; deposit of public monies; tax exempt foundations and charitable trusts; national social security, except health care and facilities programs that are supported by payroll deductions and work incentive programs; and transportation of dutiable goods. Its subcommittees include: Tax; Health; Income Security and Family Support; Oversight; Select Revenue Measures; Social Security; and, Trade.

Select Committee on Intelligence
Capitol Visitor Center
HVC - 304
US Capitol Building
Washington, DC 20515
225-7690
intelligence.house.gov

This committee has jurisdiction over the intelligence community, including the intelligence activities of the Central Intelligence Agency (CIA), Defense Intelligence Agency (DIA), National Security Agency, other agencies of DOD, and Departments of State, Justice, and Treasury. Its subcommittees include: Terrorism, HUMINT, Analysis and Counterintelligence; Technical and Tactical Intelligence; Intelligence Community Management; and Oversight.

JOINT COMMITTEES

Joint Economic Committee
G-01 Dirksen Senate Office Building
Washington, DC 20510
(202) 224-5171
jec.senate.gov

This committee is responsible for conducting studies of issues associated with the President's Economic Report and counseling members of Congress on economic issues affecting the nation. This committee has no subcommittees.

Joint Committee on Taxation
1015 Longworth House Office Building
Washington, DC. 20515
Front Office: (202) 225-3621
jct.gov

This committee is responsible for supervising the overall operation, administration, and simplification of federal tax laws and administering tax refunds in excess of $200,000. Its staff provides tax expertise for Congress and the tax-writing committees. This committee has no subcommittees.

APPENDIX B

SUGGESTED READINGS

Adler, E. Scott. 2002. *Why Congressional Reforms Fail.* Chicago: University of Chicago Press.

Baker, Ross K. 2008. *House and Senate*, 4th ed. New York: W.W. Norton

Baker, Ross K. 2007. *Strangers on a Hill: Congress and the Court.* New York: W.W. Norton.

Binder, Sarah and Steven Smith, 1997. *Politics of Principle? Filibustering in the United States Senate.* Washington, D.C.: The Brookings Institution.

Cox, Gary and Mathew McCubbins. 2005. *Setting the Agenda: Responsible Party Government in the U.S. House of Representatives.* New York: Cambridge University Press.

Davidson, Roger H. and Walter J. Oleszek. 2009. *Congress and Its Members*, 12th ed. Washington, D.C.: Congressional Quarterly Press.

Deering, Christopher and Steven S. Smith. 1997. *Committees in Congress*, 3rd ed. Washington, D.C.: Congressional Quarterly Press.

Dodd, Lawrence C. and Bruce I. Oppenheimer. 2008. *Congress Reconsidered*, 9th ed. Washington, D.C.: Congressional Quarterly Press.

Fenno, Richard F. Jr. 2003. *Going Home: Black Representatives and Their Constituents.* Chicago: University of Chicago Press.

Garber, Doris, ed. 2010. *Media Power in Politics*, 6th ed. Washington, D.C.: Congressional Quarterly Press.

Hammond, Susan Webb. 1997. *Congressional Caucuses and National Policy Making.* Baltimore: Johns Hopkins University Press.

Jacobsen, Gary. 2009. *The Politics of Congressional Elections*, 7th ed. New York: Pearson Longman.

King, David. 1997. *Turf Wars: How Congressional Committees Claim Jurisdiction*. Chicago: University of Chicago Press.

Loomis, Burdett, ed. 2000. *Esteemed Colleagues: Civility and Deliberation in the U.S. Senate*. Washington, D.C.: The Brookings Institution.

Mayhew, David R. 2004. *Congress and the Electorial Connection*, 2nd ed. New Haven: Yale University Press.

Meacham, Jon. 2009. *American Lion: Andrew Jackson in the White House*. New York: Random House.

Oleszek, Walter J. 2010. *Congressional Procedures and the Policy Process*, 8th ed. Washington, D.C.: Congressional Quarterly Press.

Ornstein, Norman and Thomas Mann. 2008. *The Broken Branch*. New York: Oxford University Press.

Schick, Allen, 2007. *The Federal Budget: Politics, Policy, and Process*, 3rd ed. Washington, D.C.: The Brookings Institution.

Sinclair, Barbara. 2007. *Unorthodox Lawmaking: New Legislative Processes in the U.S. Congress*, 3rd ed. Washington, D.C.: Congressional Quarterly Press.

Sulkin, Tracy. 2005. *Issue Politics in Congress*. New York: Cambridge University Press.

Wayne, Stephen. 2008. *The Road to the White House 2008*, 8th ed. Florence, KY: Wadsworth Publishing.

Waxman, Henry. 2010. *The Waxman Report: How Congress Really Works*. New York: Twelve.

Wilson, Woodrow. 2007. *Congressional Government*, 15th ed. Piscataway, NJ: Transaction Publishers.

APPENDIX C

Useful Telephone Numbers on Capitol Hill

(Area code is 202 for all numbers.)

General Information

Capitol Switchboard 224-3121

Status of Legislation - Status of bills and scheduled committee hearings on legislation.

Legislative Status Office (LEGIS) 225-1772

Senate Library 224-2971

Legislative Documents - Copies of bills, resolutions, calendars, committee and conference reports, and public laws may be obtained here.

Senate Document Room 224-7860

House Document Room 226-5200

Legislative Meetings/Floor Schedule - Information on legislative scheduling, meetings, floor proceedings, and congressional recess periods may be obtained here. Recorded information also provides legislative and floor schedules.

Senate Leadership Offices

Majority Leader (Republican) 224-3135

Assistant Majority Leader 224-2708

Minority Leader (Democrat) 224-5556

Minority Whip 224-2158

Recorded Information

Democratic Cloakroom 224-8541

Republican Cloakroom 224-8601

House Leadership Offices

Speaker of the House 225-0600

Majority Leader (Republican) 225-4000

Majority Whip 225-0197

Minority Leader (Democrat) 225-0100

Minority Whip 225-3130

Recorded Information - Floor Proceedings

Democratic Cloakroom 225-7400

Republican Cloakroom 225-7430

Recorded Information - Legislative Schedule

Democrat 225-1600

Republican 225-2020

GLOSSARY

LEGISLATIVE TERMS

act The term for legislation that has passed both houses of Congress and has been signed by the President, or was passed over his veto, thus becoming law.

amendment A legislator's proposal to alter the language or stipulations in a bill or act.

bill The form in which legislative proposals before Congress are introduced. Bills in the House of Representatives are designated as H.R. # and Senate bills as S. #.

budget This document, sent to Congress by the President in January each year, estimates government revenues and expenditures for the following fiscal year and recommends specific appropriations.

budget deficit The amount by which government budget outlays exceed budget receipts for a given fiscal year.

clean bill When a committee makes major changes in a bill, the chairperson usually incorporates them into what is left of the original bill and introduces a "clean bill" with a new number.

cloture The process of ending a filibuster in the Senate. Sixty senators must vote for cloture for it to be invoked, thereby ending the filibuster.

Committee of the Whole Working title of what is formally "The Committee of the Whole House of Representatives on the State of the Union." It has no fixed membership and comprises 100 members who participate in legislative debate on the floor of the House.

concurrent resolution A resolution that must pass both the House and the Senate, but does not require the President's signature, nor does it have the force of law. It is designated as S.Con.Res. or H.Con.Res.

conference The meeting between members of the House and Senate to reconcile the differences in their respective bills on a related measure.

Congressional Record The daily printed account of the procedures in both the House and Senate chambers.

continuing resolution A resolution enacted by Congress and signed by the President that allows federal agencies to continue operations until their regular appropriations bills are enacted.

engrossed bill The final copy of a bill that has passed the House or the Senate. The text amended by floor action is incorporated into the bill.

enrolled bill The final copy of a bill that has been passed in identical form by both the House and the Senate.

filibuster Prolonged debate by a senator or senators in the minority to delay a vote on a bill that probably would pass if brought to a vote.

germane Pertaining to the subject matter of the measure at hand.

hearings Committee session for hearing witnesses' testimony.

House Calendar A listing for action by the House of Representatives of all public bills that do not pertain to tax appropriations.

joint committee A committee composed of a specified number of representatives and senators for special policy studies.

joint resolution A resolution that must pass both the House and Senate, receive the President's signature, and has the force of law if so approved.

majority leader Chief strategist and floor leader for the party in control of either the House or the Senate.

majority whip The assistant majority leader in both the House and the Senate.

markup Refers to a process by which congressional subcommittees and committees revise a bill before reporting it to full committee or to the full House or Senate, respectively.

minority leader Floor leader for the minority party.

minority whip Chief assistant to the minority leader.

override A process whereby Congress annuls, or overrides, a presidential veto of a bill. It requires a two-thirds vote in each house of Congress.

pocket veto An action of the President in withholding his approval of a bill after Congress has adjourned either for the year or for a specified period.

president of the Senate The chief presiding officer of this chamber, also the U.S. vice president.

president pro tempore The chief officer in the Senate in the absence of the Senate president. He or she is usually the oldest member of the majority party.

public law A measure that has passed both houses of Congress and has been signed by the President. Laws are listed numerically by Congress; for example, Public Law 90-365 indicates that the bill was passed by the 90th Congress. It is often abbreviated as P.L.

recorded vote A vote upon which each member's stand is individually made known.

resolution A measure passed only by the chamber that introduced it. S.Res. or H.Res. deals with business pertaining only to one house or the other.

rider An unrelated measure attached to a congressional bill to compel the President to accept the bill with its rider. The President cannot veto part of a bill.

rule This term has two congressional meanings. A rule, as listed in the

House or Senate handbook, states how House and Senate business should be conducted. Secondly it means the procedure established by the House Rules Committee for floor debate on a bill.

sequestration This term refers to the automatic budget-cutting mechanism called for in a given fiscal year.

supplemental appropriations Considered after passage of regular (annual) appropriations bills. They are acted on before the end of the fiscal year to which they apply.

teller vote Used in the House, but not in the Senate, to record the totals of yeas and nays and not how the members voted individually.

unanimous consent Used in lieu of a vote on noncontroversial motions, amendments, or bills.

Union Calendar A House calendar containing bills that directly or indirectly appropriate money or raise revenue.

veto An action by the President to reject a bill passed by Congress.

views and estimates Reports prepared by House and Senate standing committees on a President's budget request for a given fiscal year that are submitted by them to the budget committees to assist in developing the budget resolution.